LONDON
1862

1 John Stubbs, Brownlow Street, Holborn, 1818
2 Antony Bazzoni, High Holborn, 1852
3 Chas. Butler, Clerkenwell, 1834
4 Soho Bazaar: various stallholders
5 Douglas & Hamer, Shoe Lane, 1844
6 Montanari, Upper Charlotte Street, Fitzroy Square, 1852
7 Charles Marsh, Fitzroy Square, 1864
8 Madame Tussaud's Waxworks, Marylebone Road
9 William Rich, Great Russell Street, 1853
10 Charles and Henrietta Edwards, Goodge Street, 1853
11 Pierotti, "The Crystal Palace," Oxford Street, 1853
12 Richard Napoleon Montanari, Rathbone Place, 1870
13 Peacock's "The Beaming Nurse," New Oxford Street, 1862
14 Hamley's Toy Shop, Regent Street, 1890
15 Corinthian Bazaar, Argyll Street
16 Joseph Evans' Toy Warehouse, Newgate Street, 1827
17 Linwood Gallery (Montanari), Leicester Square, 1855
18 Pantheon Bazaar, Oxford Street
19 Mrs Lucy Peck, "The Dolls' Home," Regent Street, 1890
20 Cremer's Toyshop, Regent Street, 1862
21 Morell's Toy Shop, Burlington Arcade, Piccadilly
22 H.J. Meech & Sons, Kennington Road
23 John Edwards' factory, Waterloo Road, 1868
24 Wheelhouse works, Waterloo Road, 1857
25 Lowther Arcade, Strand

THE HISTORY OF
WAX DOLLS
MARY HILLIER

THE HISTORY OF
WAX DOLLS
MARY HILLIER

Published By  HOBBY HOUSE PRESS, INC.
Cumberland, Maryland 21502

First published in the United States in 1985 by Hobby House Press Inc, 900 Frederick Street, Cumberland, Maryland 21502. (301) 759-3770.

ISBN: 0-87588-237-4

Created, designed and produced by Black Pig Editions Ltd (Justin Knowles Publishing Group), P.O. Box 99, Exeter, Devon, England.

Editor: Christopher Pick
Design: Tim Harvey
Production: Nick Facer

Typeset by P & M Typesetting Ltd, Exeter, England
Printed and bound in Hong Kong by Mandarin Offset Ltd

First American Edition

The publishers gratefully acknowledge the following who supplied photographic material for this book:

Alberici Cesare 18, 21; Mrs Marianne Bodmer 17, 32, 33, 68, 72, 94 (left); British Museum 11 (far right); Dean and Chapter of Westminster 23; Michael Dowty 122; Glyptothek, Munich 11 (left); Mrs Graham Greene 142; Guildhall Library 71 (centre); Hawkley Studio Associates Ltd 8,9 (top and bottom), 12, 13, 14, 15 (left), 16, 25, 28, 36, 37 (left, centre and right), 40, 45, 51, 53, 56, 57, 60, 61, 66 (top), 69, 76, 77, 78 (top, centre and bottom), 80, 83, 84, 85, 87, 88, 90 (right), 95, 96, 97, 100, 101, 102 (top left), 104, 105 (bottom), 107, 108, 109, 111, 112, 113, 114, 115, 116, 117, 121, 124, 125, 134; Mary Hillier 54, 70, 106, 128, 146; Manchester Public Libraries 102 (right); Richard Merrill 27, 30, 40, 43, 46, 49, 82, 90 (left), 91 (right and far right), 93; Museum of London 29, 41 (bottom), 44, 64, 81, 89, 92, 120; Nantucket Historical Association 55; Mrs Norman-Smith 134, 136, 137, 138, 139, 141, 143, 151; Pollock's Toy Museum 66 (bottom); E.J. Pyke 26 (top and bottom); Rijksmuseum, Amsterdam 42; Rowan Studios Ltd 132 (left and right); Royal Library, Windsor 140 (top); Shelburne Museum, Vermont 71 (far right); Somerset County Museum, Taunton 58; Sotheby's London 15 (right), 41 (top), 98 (top), 118, 123; Sperryn's Ltd 31; Windsor Spice 67, 129 (top); State Historical Society of Wisconsin 126, 127; Graham Strong 48, 52, 65; Sudbury Hall 73, 94 (right), 110; Derrick Witty 10, 47, 119; Worthing Museum and Art Gallery 75, 99; Westminster City Library Archives Dept. 91 (bottom).

Frontispiece "Violet," thought to have been bought in a Paris shop by an American for his young niece. (State Historical Society of Wisconsin)

Contents

Publisher's Note

Following the interest in an exhibition of wax dolls at one of London's Toy and Doll shows, I became aware of the limited bibliography on the interesting and important subject of the history of wax dolls.

It is often the case that collectors and even specialist dealers cannot thoroughly research or fully articulate their subject; it takes a special person, such as expert researcher and writer Mary Hillier, who has a strong feeling for a subject to do a chosen topic justice. As a long-standing admirer of Mary Hillier's work, I was more than encouraged when she expressed a special interest in wax dolls – an interest that has now resulted in the publication of this book.

Intended as the first of a series on doll subjects, we believe that this definitive work is a major and classic contribution to the wax doll subject. We thank Mary Hillier for her great efforts on the preparation of the book and Gary Ruddell and Chris Revi at Hobby House Press Inc. for their co-publishing commitment and shared interest in the subject.

Justin Knowles
Black Pig Editions, London 1985

Acknowledgements

On the endpapers of this book is printed a section of an 1862 map of London, originally supplied with a guide to the Exhibition of that year. It was produced at the period when many important makers of wax dolls were working, and the sites of their homes and the shops and bazaars where their goods were sold may be traced. It is possible, in a car, to tour them all in a morning, for they were concentrated in a fairly limited area. In my writing I have tried to add substance to some of those shadowy names of the past whose work was so much admired and is still eagerly collected. I have sought to bring alive the London scene which promoted their success. I hope the reader will enjoy this story and the light it throws on an industry which lasted really a very short time: the making of that favourite Victorian plaything, the wax doll. Especially, I have tried to show the importance of the Royal Model Baby doll and the influence that the large family of Queen Victoria had in providing a pattern for baby dolls.

A book of this sort is not achieved without the encouragement and information of a wide circle of friends, collectors and museum curators. I would like to thank all those who have helped me in my research, lent dolls and photographs and showed interest in my theories! More facts will come to light eventually and more fine examples will illustrate the doll gallery. I am especially indebted to: Marianne Bodmer, Zurich; Heather Bond; Betty Cadbury and the authorities of Sudbury Hall; Bunny Campione, Sotheby's, London; Dorothy S. Coleman; Faith Eaton; Jo Clay Gerken; M. A. V. Gill of Tunbridge Wells Museum; Margaret Glover; Caroline Goodfellow at the Bethnal Green Museum, London; Vivien Greene; Lorna Liebemann of Wenham Museum, Massachusetts; Joan Severa, Historical Museum, Wisconsin; Betty Simson for the loan of her precious "Tussaud" baby; Kay Staniland of the Museum of London. I owe an especial debt to E.J. Pyke for allowing me to draw on his definitive book on wax modellers, *A Biographical Dictionary of Wax Modellers* (Oxford University Press, 1973). Readers interested in the historical background should consult this book. I am also grateful for the interest and help of various existing descendants of doll-making families: Miss Irene Pierotti, Mrs Norman-Smith (grand-daughter of Mrs Lucy Peck) and several members of the Meech and Edwards families.

Finally, I should like to thank my photographers for both their skill and co-operation: Richard Merrill (Saugus, Massachusetts, U.S.A.), Nick Nicholson (Hawkley Studio Associates Ltd), Graham Strong and Derrick Witty.

Below Alice with a Valentine. This pretty mid-19th century poured wax doll wears a very charming printed muslin dress patterned in brown and a brown straw hat to match. Alice wears a locket and also carries the original hand-designed Valentine. Was the doll given to a child or to a girl of riper years? The verse reads:

You sweet little pet
I like you so much
If you'll be my wife
I'll have you as such.

Sadly no more history is forthcoming, but the doll has been carefully preserved and does not show signs of having been played with, so perhaps it became a romantic souvenir. 19-20 inches. (Tunbridge Wells Museum)

The Origins of Wax-Modelling

Above Rock-painting from the Cuevas De La Arana, Spain, depicting a Neolithic gatherer of wild honey. After an original copy made by "W.K." (1921)

Above Egyptian wall-painting scene from the tomb of Rekhmi-Re at Thebes showing an offering of honeycomb. (Metropolitan Museum of Art, New York)

"'Begin at the beginning,' the King said gravely, 'and go on till you come to the end: then stop.'" (*Alice in Wonderland*, Lewis Carroll) Now, Alice in Wonderland, as a child of her age, would no doubt have been fully aware of Victorian poured wax dolls. She lived (or was invented) in the heyday of the craft, the middle years of the 19th century, when the finest wax dolls were being produced. (Lewis Carroll's famous book was published in 1865.) This book deals primarily with such dolls and their makers, but to set the scene for Alice and any others interested one has to return to the beginning, to the primary material: beeswax.

The first serious apiculture seems to have taken place in Egypt. After the excavation at Sakkara at the end of the 19th century, wall paintings in a temple were discovered which depicted well-organized *apiarii* with teams of men emptying the hives, filling and sealing container jars with honey and even carrying decorative dishes laden with honeycomb. Tomb finds have revealed that wax was used for fashioning some of the Ushabti (servants of the dead intended to act as surrogate attendants in the after-world), and both honey and wax were used in embalming.

Most early civilizations looked upon honey as sacred and bees of divine origin. The translation of a curious Egyptian papyrus in the British Museum reads:

> The god Re wept and the tears from his eyes fell on the ground and turned into a bee.
> The bee made his comb and busied himself with the flowers of every plant;
> So wax was made and also honey out of the tears of the god Re.

This may all seem remote from our subject, but both practical methods of bee-farming and the beliefs connected with bees and honey had a direct influence on European wax-modelling.

The Egyptians are also credited with discovering the *cire perdue* or 'lost wax' method of bronze sculpture casting, and they also fashioned waxen effigies of their gods. The Greeks and Romans, who learnt about bee-keeping from Egyptian colonists, both made wax portraits and used encaustic methods for painting with coloured wax. They created wax busts of their ancestors' likenesses, and it must be believed children's dolls as well, since they made dolls from wood, clay and fabric. Since wax is a more delicate material, examples have not survived.

With the advent of Christianity the mystic nature of the bee and its products seems to have been adopted by the Church. "The origin of Bees is from Paradise and on account of the sin of man they came hence, and God conferred his blessing upon them and therefore the Mass cannot be said without wax", according to one manuscript dating from AD 950. In fact

9

Opposite German needlework doll with wax face on wood, tiny black glass eyes, real hair, and a wood body with peg-jointed arms and legs. She is wearing a silk check skirt, and fringed silk overskirt. *C.*1860. 13 inches. (Bethnal Green Museum of Childhood)

Right Marble gravestone of a dollmaker from Attica, 320-10 BC. 30 inches. (Glyptothek, Munich)

Far right Bronze figure from Pompeii of Bacchus as a child, made by the *cire perdue* method. Images and doll-like figures of children were popular in classical times, and were often tokens of boy-worship or had a religious significance. Sometimes they were actually moulded from wax.

> Tell me gentle youth I pray thee
> What in purchase shall I pay thee
> For this little waxen toy
> Image of the Paphian boy?

(Odes of Anacreon, Ode XI, translated by Thomas Moore)
Old Paphias, on the west coast of Cyprus, was the chief centre of the worship of Aphrodite, who is said to have landed there after her birth among the waves. The temple was dedicated to her, and the image mentioned in the Ode would be a love symbol, as Eros was her son. (British Museum)

holiness was attributed to bee colonies because they were believed to owe their existence to virgin birth, and indeed the life of the hive was held up as a model of industry and good order.

For centuries only beeswax was permitted for the making of church candles, the pure liquid wax being run down long wicks until successive coats had produced enough thickness. The art of apiculture was improved in the monasteries and convents, and besides candles for the Mass wax was used for votive objects, encouraging clever carving and modelling. Churches in the devout areas of Italy and southern Germany became unbelievably crowded with wax images of hands, legs, eyes left by people pleading for divine intercession in their illness. The famous Surauer family of Wasserburg in Austria were renowned for the votive waxes they made from wooden moulds, using pear, walnut and plum tree wood. Developed in the mid-16th century, the art was passed from father to son unbroken to the last years of the 19th century. The art of modelling characters in wax for Christmas *crèche* scenes and for larger figures such as shrine saints also originated because of Church teaching, and in later pages it will be seen how such work was connected with doll-making.

Besides the Christian belief in the sanctity of bees and their products, there was a darker side to beliefs connected with wax. Little wax effigies made by hand were employed in both black and white magic from very early times. Plato refers to wizardry and the fashioning of "love" charms, and a hundred years later the Greek poet Theocritus wrote of a spell put on a faithless lover:

> The Spirit aids, the mammet melts above
> And so may he
> Delphis, the Myndian, melt in grids of love
> As utterly ...

The sinister implication here is of witchcraft or "referred magic," by which damage or injury or even actual death was done to the replica of a

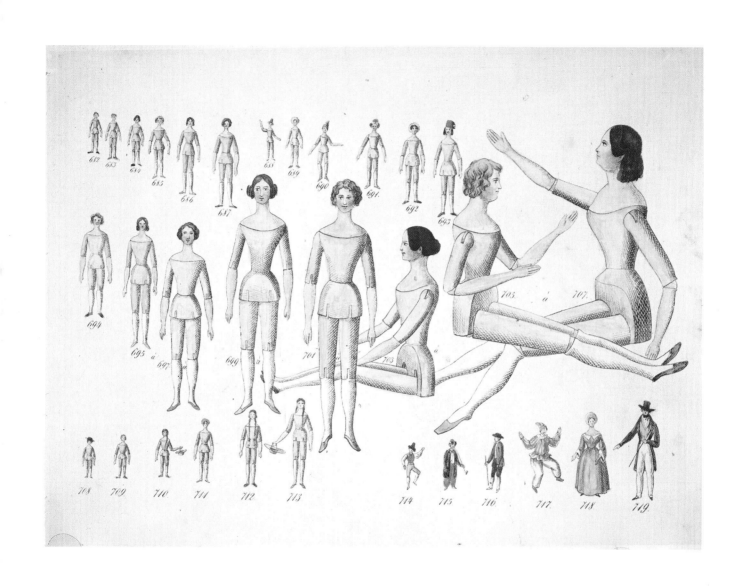

Above German doll-maker's catalogue *c.*1840 showing various types and sizes of pegged wooden dolls with wax-over heads and details of coiffeur, costume etc. (Mary Hillier)

Opposite Small German wax-over composition doll with slit hair, peg wooden body and limbs, and wire-pull eyes. Owned by a daughter of Queen Victoria. 1840/50. 10 inches. (Bethnal Green Museum of Childhood)

hated enemy. Wax was obviously a good material since it was readily obtainable, could be simply fashioned even by an amateur, and could be pierced with nails or needles, tortured or burned. When people believed in witchcraft, such actions proved very harmful and there are many records of people who became ill because they knew they were being victimized in this way. Indeed, witches responsible for such actions could be burnt or put to death. Perhaps the most famous case was in 1445, when the Duchess of Gloucester was accused of this crime against the King of England, Henry VI. She was imprisoned and her three accomplices put to death. In the 17th century many witches were accused of image magic in America, where presumably the superstition had been taken by European emigrants. The last trial for witchcraft was in 1712, but even then the practice lingered on.

As late as 1839, Lady Charlotte Bury described in her memoirs how she had witnessed the Princess of Wales, the unlovable Princess Caroline of Brunswick, make a wax figure in 1814: "As usual she gave it an amiable addition of large horns. Then she took three pins out of her garment and stuck them through and through and put the figure to roast and melt in the fire." Possibly this uncouth girl bore some recollections of traditions in her own country, and she had reason enough to bear her husband a grudge.

The study of apiculture became more scientific and eventually by the 17th century the relation of the Queen bee and drones was watched and understood. The industry of bees and their life and function within the hive was still considered an ideal model for man. On May 5, 1665, Samuel Pepys wrote in his famous diary, "After dinner to Mr Evelyn's, he being abroad, and we walked in his garden [Deptford] and a lovely noble ground he hath indeed. And among his other rarities, a hive of bees so being hived

Right Mrs Valentine's *Home Book of Pleasure and Instruction*, published in 1867, is intended for grown-up girls. Mrs Valentine suggests dressing dolls in complicated foreign costumes or as historical characters as a sort of educational ploy, but also mentions "very pretty Lady's Companions or Work-Table Friends for holding cotton, needles, thimble etc," such as the examples shown here. She lists suitable types as a *"French Cantinière* (a maid serving at a canteen or bar); a charity school girl; an old market woman with basket; a milkmaid with milk pails; an old lady with gold earrings and a mob cap." All were designed with pockets to hold the packets of pins etc. (Mrs Hutchinson)

Right In common with dolls of all sorts of other materials, including cheap German wooden ones, china and ornamental composition, small wax dolls were used to make up little characters. Especially popular were the pedlar dolls with trays of little wares – a familiar sight in 19th-century life. The characterization necessary for an old man or woman was easily achieved with pliable wax and there are home-made examples with the wax head made up and fitted on a wooden stump which could be clothed in the usual red cloak and voluminous skirts of the market woman.

The doll shown here is an illustration of a "Witch Pen-Wiper" from *Girl's Own Toy Maker*, published in London in 1860. The text reads:

"Procure a brown wax doll, with an old woman's face if possible. Fix something on the back to give the appearance of stooping and fold some cloth round the legs to serve for petticoats and also for the purpose of wiping the pen. Put on an old fashioned cotton skirt and for the cloak cut out a piece of red cloth, rather longer than the breadth, and a shoulder piece of the same material and gather the cloak on to this; then cut out a cape long enough to cover the shoulders; sew this round the neck of the latter piece, bind it neatly, and also the cloak; tie round the neck a small red ribbon, first having cut

out two holes for the arms. Quill up some narrow lace for a cap, and make a large bonnet of black satin, with a high old-fashioned crown, then put in the cap, rather near the edge of the bonnet, sewing it on to the head of the doll. Get a small basket, line it with pink glazed calico, and fill it up with small pincushions, &c. and hang it on the arm of the old woman. In the hand place a small twig for a stick. When completed it will make a pretty and useful ornament for a

writing table or, if very neatly executed, they form a pretty embellishment for the chimney piece or side table. (Mary Hillier)

Above English wax pedlar doll. 1850. 9 inches. (Sotheby's)

in glass you may see the bees making their honey and combs mighty pleasantly." The spirit of the age was scientific enquiry, and this was reflected also in the skills of those who were using wax as an artistic medium and perfecting methods of portrait-making which were the true origin of simple doll-making.

Old superstitions gradually faded as the public became more educated. Throughout the 17th and 18th centuries in Europe, crowds would wonder at medical and anatomical exhibitions, often demonstrating working organs. Museums sprang up displaying automata and waxworks of celebrated historic personages. For many of these popular and ingenious displays the skills of the wax-modeller were in demand, and it was from these origins that the specialist art of the wax doll as a child's plaything eventually evolved.

WORK-TABLE COMPANION

Expressly designed for the

'Englishwoman's Domestic Magazine'

Above Pattern for a needlework doll to be used as a "worktable companion" for pins, needles etc from the *Englishwoman's Domestic Magazine*, 1860. (Mary Hillier)

Opposite English wax pedlar doll. 1810. 10 inches. (Mrs Marianne Bodmer, Zurich)

Life-Size Wax Portrait Models

The art of making fine life-sized wax portraits of notable characters seems to have originated in 15th-century Italy. Real human hair was used for the wigs, beautiful blown glass eyes were added and the features tinted and tooled to imitate the subject, whose actual clothing, jewellery and accoutrements were used to promote realism.

Giorgio Vasari, writing in 1550 in *The Lives of the Most Excellent Italian Architects, Painters and Sculptors*, commented that "The art, although it has remained alive up to our own time, is nevertheless on the decline." He was in a good position to judge, since fine effigies that have long since been destroyed could still be seen in churches. The Benintendi family of Florence, for instance, was renowned for such work over several generations. Vasari relates that Orsini Benintendi was helped by none less than the painter Andrea del Verrocchio (1435-88), the pupil of Donatello and master of Leonardo, when he made three life-size models of the famous Lorenzo de' Medici. Lorenzo was wounded in an assassination attempt in 1478 in which his brother was killed, and the models were set up as thanksgivings to God for his survival. One model was actually represented with the throat bandaged to indicate his wound. Benintendi's technique was described by Vasari:

> He made the skeleton within of wood, interwoven with split reeds, which were then covered with waxed cloths folded and arranged so beautifully that nothing better or more true to nature could be seen. Then he made the heads, hands and feet with wax of greater thickness, but hollow within, portrayed from life, and painted in oils with all the ornaments of hair and everything that was necessary, so lifelike and well wrought that they seemed no mere images of wax, but actual living men.

One must conclude from this that the artist was using a poured wax method after sculpting a likeness in clay. It is especially interesting to note that he used waxed clothes. A similar method was employed in some of the earliest miniature *crèche* scenes, the applied layer of wax preserving the folds of material in position and keeping them from rotting.

Other famous artists of the Renaissance used wax for a variety of reasons. Leonardo himself (1452-1519), an innovator in so many fields, is said to have been the first to experiment with realistic anatomical models to illustrate the functions of the human body. Wax could be tooled and coloured and had an uncanny resemblance to the texture of skin and human tissue. Verrocchio learnt construction skills from the Benintendi workshop. The great Benvenuto Cellini, master of metal work, described in his notebooks how he used wax for the *cire perdue* method in casting both very large and quite small metal work. Famous work from his hand survives, including Perseus with the Medusa's head and exquisite portrait medallions. Cellini did not always keep on the side of the law, and he recounts with some glee how when he was locked up in prison he taught other inmates to fashion false keys for their cells by taking wax impressions!

The sculptor Michelangelo worked with wax for small plans of his bigger statues, and like Cellini he used large quantities for casting bronze. In a letter in which he recorded buying 720 lb wax, he is triumphant at having acquired it at a bargain price and comments: "It is not the nature of these Bolognese to take a *quattrino* less than they ask." Throughout the 16th century, artists were experimenting with and innovating fine work. A school of modelling the beautiful shrine and *crèche* figures in polychrome wax much in demand for churches was established in the district around Naples, and an increasing number of artists from Bologna worked on wax figure portraiture.

It was in Bologna that Angelo Pio (1690-1769) introduced the art of making realistic wax portrait models. He used glass eyes, inserted real hair and dressed his dolls in actual costume and belongings to give a true air of authenticity. Pio can justly be thought of as one of the fathers of the waxwork, for his methods of depicting his subject "to the life" were later adopted by many others. He was a pupil of Ferrari, who had founded the school of life-size model-making of famous people. It is evident that there was a consecutive practice, the skills being handed on, just as in the Pierotti family of doll-makers (see pages 74-82), to following generations. More important than Pio, it is intriguing to find, was the very famous woman sculptor Anna Morandi (1716-74). Born in Bologna, she was early apprenticed to a studio where she learned drawing and sculpture. She met her husband Giovanni Manzolini, another artist, there and was married in 1740. Both of them worked with Ercole Lelli, who became famous for his anatomical models when he collaborated with a Bolognese medical school. Realizing how important this work was for medical research, the Archbishop of Bologna, when he became Pope Benedetto XIV, commissioned the team to supply a complete museum collection of the models at his own expense. Manzolini died in 1755 and Benedetto XIV then gave Anna an income for life. She achieved enormous fame for her brilliant work, which, on account of its high patronage, has fortunately all been preserved in the Science Academy. Manzolini is credited with having invented a secret process of making the wax more durable and using life-like colours. The work is impressive and eerie, so close to reality that we are shocked by the depiction of the naked new-born baby with umbilical cord and placenta attached, though it has to be remembered how valuable such teaching aids were to the medical profession of that time.

The collection was installed in its fine building in 1776, and the beautiful self-portrait busts of Anna Morandi and her husband are handsomely encased on the walls where they can survey their handiwork with justifiable pride. The convolutions of brains, the interiors of ears and the construction of eyes and nerves were shown in details copied from intimate dissections. The work was done with incredible skills that were presently to be employed in European waxwork displays and in the production of those many life-like figures who, as was often said, "only lacked breath" to complete their realism.

Anna Morandi received invitations from all over Europe and from Russia to visit and teach her skill, but she always refused. None the less, her influence must have caused many others to emulate her work; and anatomical-pathological collections not only became an academic requirement for instruction but were also found intriguing, even titillating, by the general public.

Wax apparatus devised by surgeons to illustrate the function of the internal organs or the vascular system of blood flow was ingenious and beautifully made. Originally intended for instruction, it was eventually placed in museums. The Ruysch Museum in Amsterdam with anatomical work by the Dutchman Frederick Ruysch (1638-1731) was highly thought of by Peter the Great, who bought it in its entirety in 1717. The famous Philippe Curtius who taught Madame Tussaud her art was himself a doctor who first practised wax modelling for anatomical models in the 1760 period (see page 51).

In 18th-century London there were various exhibitions of this type of work. The surgeon Desnoues showed his work at Rackstrow's Museum before it was bought for the University of Dublin. Benjamin Rackstrow (c. 1717-72) himself established his Statuary in London at Fleet Street in 1746, and it was famous until he died. One of the chief attractions was a wax model of a woman eight months pregnant. The handbill advertised that the action of the heart and lungs and the flow of blood could be clearly witnessed, so one imagines it was also a mechanical figure. Other items sound to have been rather more unwholesome and the advertising, which announced that ladies and gentlemen were conducted separately, hints at the general tone of this public exhibition. Rackstrow's show was a popular one which included all sorts of curiosities besides his anatomical models. There were true waxwork representations of freaks such as a famous dwarf

Right Examples of anatomical wax works made by the Manzolini family including limbs and dissections. (Instituto di Anatomia Umana Normale, Bologna)

and a giant. In these he entered into competition with the other famous Fleet Street waxworks run by Mrs Salmon (see below).

It is difficult in these days of full media coverage to imagine what a revelation an old-fashioned waxwork was to the throng who viewed it. Here, large as life, in replica of costume and style they could see the great personages of the day, legendary leaders like Oliver Cromwell or, later, Wellington, Nelson and Napoleon, heroes from the past and royalty. At the other end of the scale, they could shudder at the images of rogues, thieves and murderers, villains who curdled the blood just as the gutter press or video nasties do today.

The Swiss Johann Schalch (1623-1704) presented one of the first London waxwork exhibitions in 1685. Schalch travelled a great deal in Europe and was famous for his optical apparatus and making glass eyes. He worked for royalty and in 1694 made a death mask of Queen Mary. He also showed a scene which portrayed the death bed of Mary Stuart. He was a true showman who liked to lecture to his public and with becoming modesty described himself as "The Eighth Wonder of the World."

During the 18th century many travelling waxworks toured the country in the fashion later practised by the famous Madame Tussaud, but enjoying less publicity. Very often a woman's name is associated with them, and one suspects that it was essential for a woman to be involved in the team to do the sewing, repairs and the display.

One of the characters we wish we knew more about is Mrs Salmon (1650-1740), who advertised herself as a toy-maker and wax-modeller. Her premises were first near St Martin's and then in Fleet Street. It is said that Thomas Besnier, a young sculptor born in England of French parents, made some of the first models shown by her and her husband, but he died young in 1693. After Mr Salmon died in 1718 she remarried, and as Mrs Steers ran her own show. Did she perhaps also make dolls as a sideline? She advertised that she could supply moulds and glass eyes and teach "the full art." Her tableaux sound truly eccentric and included "Margaret, Countess of Heningbergh, Lying on a Bed of State, with her Three Hundred and Sixty Five Children, all born at one birth, and baptized by the names of Johns and Elizabeths, occasioned by the rash Wish of a poor beggar Woman!" That the show was amusing is vouched for by the artist William Hogarth, who remembered that as an apprentice "he frequently loitered at old Mother Salmon's to take a peep at the humorous pieces." How one might wish he had depicted the scene. After Mrs Salmon's death, her waxworks were shown by a Mrs Clark until she died in 1812, and finally the items were lost and some were stolen and destroyed.

Mrs Salmon had a permanent exhibition, but there were many travelling waxworks after the style of the famous concern described by Dickens in *The Old Curiosity Shop*, who had no doubt witnessed one. One of the best known before the arrival of Madame Tussaud (who is dealt with separately on page 51) was the Royal Waxwork of an Irish couple, Mr and Mrs Sylvester. They worked in Dublin and Edinburgh between 1780 and 1794, but were variously recorded in Hull, Norwich and London. Besides models of a full-length Sleeping Venus and such notables as Franklin, Voltaire and the Royal Family of France, they advertised that they would execute work on the spot: "Any Lady or Gentleman who may wish to have a likeness in Wax will please to apply at the Place of Exhibition," and, a claim that

Right Life-size models of Katherine, Duchess of Buckingham (d. 1743) and her son, Robert, Marquess of Normandy. Unknown modeller. (The Westminster Abbey Collection)

Opposite This curious group of five wax heads and an assortment of hands came up as a lot in a doll auction, although clearly they originally had had some quite other purpose. All are mounted on sturdy wooden pegs which bear old labels with a hand-written "Nelson" and a number. The moulded hands have the remnants of fabric cuffs, so maybe there was a body clothed in fabric with its character completed by wax head and hands. The important clue that reveals their identity is the long well-shaped naked arm with a hand clasping its wrist. I am sure that originally this group depicted the death-bed scene of Nelson in the cockpit of the orlap deck of the *Victory*. The famous picture painted by Arthur William Davis in 1806, shown on the **right,** when *Victory* returned with the Admiral's body after Trafalgar, hangs at the National Maritime Museum, Greenwich.

The characters around the dying man have been identified, and this small waxwork would have been carefully constructed to represent the scene. Sadly, the central figure of Nelson is missing, but the others three have brown eyes and two blue, and two of the heads have grey hair. In the original picture, other characters crowd in anxiously at the sides, but the central group lit by a lantern was probably all that the modeller attempted. It looks as though the group was a travelling show, and that each head was removable with a wooden stump numbered to fit into a body socket. Each head measures about 5 inches, the arms 8 inches. There is inserted human hair and glass eyes, as in poured wax dolls.

It is intriguing to discover that in 1891, when the Royal Naval Exhibition was staged in the grounds of the Royal Military Hospital, Chelsea, a full-sized waxwork depiction of *The Death of Nelson* was modelled by none less than John Theodore Tussaud, grandson of Madame Tussaud. The group also included a small cameo wax of Nelson himself and another of an early 19th-century

statesman. The group was placed in a full-size model of *HMS Victory*, with the ship's timbers and lamplight lending drama to the scene. A contemporary report in the *Illustrated London News* says rather sourly that this was "an effect too realistic and sensational for refined taste. It would have perhaps been more agreeable, instead of this ghastly waxworks, to have borrowed the fine picture itself." The blood-stained uniform and the waxwork pallor must have caught the hearts of the visiting throng; then, as now, the hero of Trafalgar was a name to conjure with. This original little waxwork

goes further back in time, and I wish I knew its history. As in the painting, the heads are well characterized: Captain Hardy at the back, grey-haired and compassionate; Dr Scott, the chaplain, rubbing Nelson's chest; the purser Mr Busby, supporting the pillow of the dying man; and, most touchingly, Chevallier, Nelson's faithful steward, grey-haired and anxiously turning for reassurance to the Surgeon Dr Beatty, who holds Nelson's wrist to test his pulse. In the *Illustrated London News* engraving, a sailor is included holding the lamp. (Heads and hands – Mary Hillier)

showed some confidence in their skill, "Should the portraits not be thought the most striking and correct Likeness, the proprietor would expect nothing for his trouble."

It is amusing to learn that when the sculptor Joseph Nollekins was required to do some repairs at Westminster Abbey in about 1780, he enquired about what was considered one of the oldest waxwork shows in the world: the "Ragged Regiment", as they were called by Westminster schoolboys. He objected that money was charged for seeing them and suggested he would rather visit Mrs Salmon. These particular effigies were indeed very ancient. It was the custom in the past when a king or queen

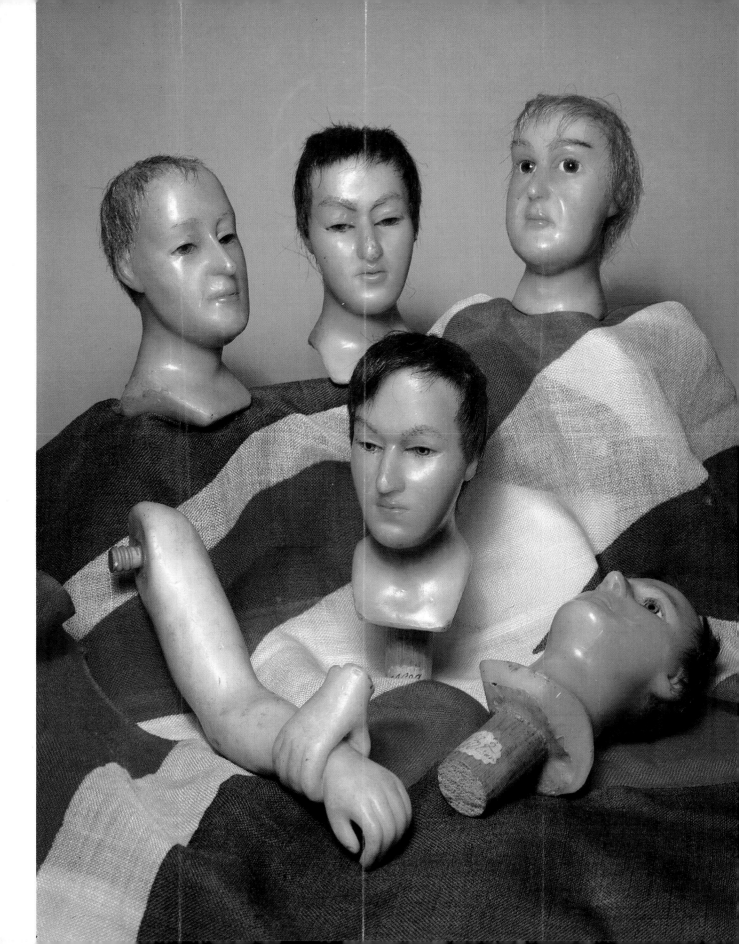

Above Portrait of Charlotte, Princess of Wales, in wax by Samuel Percy, 1817, in the original carved and gilded frame. (E.J. Pyke)

Above Wax model by Richard Cockle Lucas of the Marchioness of Blandford. 1832. 18 inches. (E.J. Pyke)

died to take a plaster death mask and then make a life-size effigy with wax features and hands and clothed in finery. This could be used for a lying-in-state on a black-clad platform called a "herse," which would be carried with the coffin at the final funeral procession. As some of these effigies had lain neglected in the Abbey since the 14th century (including the one of Edward III, who died in 1377) and others had been stolen, they were in a ruined state, and Nollekens thought they should be discarded. None the less they were retained and may be seen today. After the Second World War they were disinterred and major rescue and restoration work took place in 1949. It was then attested that human hair had been used for these early models; their bodies had a finely carved wooden framework, and the remaining fragments proved that the bodies had been stuffed out with straw or sea-grass. Experts injected preservative solutions to hold together crumbling plaster and cleaned off the centuries-old dirt. Bringing the effigies back to life was a moving experience and they now parade proudly with such later models as the figure of Nelson by Catherine Andras and the beautiful wax portraits of William III and Mary II made by Mrs Goldsmith, who also made the Duchess of Richmond by a special bequest in that lady's will in 1702.

In the 18th century, the art of the modeller of wax portraits was in heavy demand and artists of real talent enjoyed a very fashionable success. One of the most famous, Joachim Smith, who designed for the potter Josiah Wedgwood, was commissioned by Queen Caroline to make a tiny model of her new-born son, the Prince of Wales, later George IV. She kept the model on her toilet table and it was described in the *London Chronicle* in 1763 as:

> A whole length model, naked, about four inches lying on a couch of crimson velvet in the manner of an infant undresst: his left leg drawn up and his right stretched out, his right arm he holds upwards, his left lies down by his side in which he holds his shirt which is supposed to be slippt off from his right arm and lies carelessly about him.

The pretty statuette was protected by a glass dome bell and was made in natural colours "not painted, but blended and incorporated to diffuse the various tints and softness of nature." This treasure seems to have been lost, but a cameo remains which attests to the artist's skill. It shows the little Prince of Wales at about three years old and is in the Royal Collection still.

A further aspect of the commercial side of wax-modelling was shown by an advertisement published by the celebrated artist Samuel Percy (1750-1820) when he was passing through the fashionable town of Tunbridge Wells *en route* for Brighton in 1787.

> Mr. Percy, Modeller of Stained Wax, respectfully informs the nobility and gentry that he has now arrived and shall receive orders for likenesses for a short time on his way to Brighthelmstone [Brighton] at the Great Room of the Walks, where numbers of specimens may be seen of Subjects taken from life and after demise, his abilities being so well known in this County and the Kingdom at large it is unnecessary in this puffing age to spin out his own Panegyric further than to acquaint the Nobility and Gentry in general.

It may be noted Percy was still a young man and highly successful. His work was exquisite and he charged one and a half guineas for a coloured wax profile and one guinea for a plain white. He also made beautiful tableaux with the figures complete. Especially fine is the portrait of the ill-fated Princess Charlotte who would have become Queen of England had she not died in childbirth in 1817. The wax must have been made that very year as the tell-tale curve of her green and gold wax dress indicates that she was pregnant (see opposite).

It is interesting to note that Percy used his own, unique method for portraiture. The secret of his accuracy was that he carved a likeness in hard wax direct from the sitter and then made a mould of plaster-of-paris, into which were pressed the various tinted wax details of flesh, hair, dress and accessories. Then the mould was filled with liquid wax. When it had solidified, the portrait could be finished by hand, and if required further copies could be taken from the original mould. Occasionally tiny glass beads and pearls were used to represent jewellery and touches of lace or flowers were added to complete the illusion. The existence of moulds meant that fakes could later be made if they fell into unscrupulous hands. There was no doubt a ready market for some of the inferior likenesses turned out of a popular hero like Nelson.

During the late years of the 18th century and the beginning of the 19th, many famous wax-modellers lived in the Soho district of London. Some were involved in portraiture, others designed coins and medals, and yet others like John Flaxman (1755-1826) designed classical cameos and portrait medallions for the famous Wedgwood pottery works. Some of them, like the Gosset family, were of French Huguenot origin; London attracted many foreign artists because of the high patronage and fashionable shops it offered.

Wax-modelling obviously became a popular hobby among ladies of the nobility during this period. Young Anne Seymour Conway (1749-1828) was

Right 18th-century wax shoulder head, with a detail **far right**. This was obviously a figure from a religious scene, and was perhaps made in an Italian nunnery. The body is constructed of wire over a central stick support, and the wax hands and feet are finely modelled. The head is a solid dome, the eyelids are downcast and contemplative. The eyes are painted black, the hair is decorated with a circlet of coloured glass beads, and the silk costume is trimmed with metallic gold lace and a necklet of beads. Coloured thread flowers decorate the hem of the robe. 13 inches. (Maury Collection, Wenham Museum, Massachusetts)

Above Wax infant model made up into an actual death mask, and wearing a beautiful robe embroidered with the coat of arms of Don Santia Gode. *C.*1690. The custom of modelling the last member of a noble family was said to be prevalent in the Iberian peninsula. 25 inches. (Bethnal Green Museum of Childhood)

Opposite Child model wearing dress of Spitalfields silk, with decoration in silver wire and spangles, and red wax high-heeled shoes. The dress has "leading strings" as for a child. English. 10 inches. (Museum of London)

Right Boy's head in wax with glass eyes and applied hair in tinted wax. Italian. 1810. 18 inches. (Sotheby's)

Opposite This wax doll, which was probably made in Italy, has a well-modelled head with inset black glass eyes and a brown wig, a stuffed cloth body and wax hands. It is wearing its original clothes: white night shift, blue and white striped satin gown, scarlet calimanco "Turkish" dressing-gown trimmed with silver braid, and red knitted woollen stockings with a spare pair to hand. The head is cracked, the right hand damaged and the left hand missing. 23 inches. (Wenham Museum, Massachusetts)

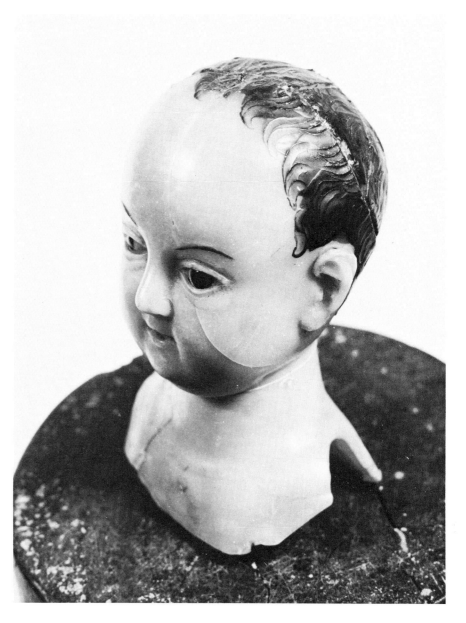

noticed at the age of 14 modelling in wax and later, as Mrs Damer, earned quite a name for her skill, exhibiting at the Royal Academy. When she died she asked for her tools to be buried with her. Even more famous in her day was Patience Wright (1725-86), who was said to have been the first wax-modeller in America. She set up an exhibition of wax figures in New York City in 1771 but later, after a fire, transferred to London. Walpole mentioned her in 1775 in a letter:

> And apropos of puppets, there is a Mrs Wright arrived from America to make figures in wax of Lord Chatham, Lord Lyttelton and Mrs Macaulay. Lady Aylesbury literally spoke to a waxen figure of a housemaid in the room, for the artistress has brought over a group and Mrs Fitzroy's aunt is one of them.

Below and opposite Two views of a dolls'
courtyard. 17th century. (Mrs Marianne
Bodmer, Zurich)

Late 17th-century Italian or Spanish wax doll. The head is realistically modelled and has brown glass eyes, and there is a stuffed cloth body with wax hands. The doll is wearing her original costume, which consists of a whitework petticoat, a cerise spotted silk underskirt, and a sky-blue moiré silk dress trimmed with silver braid, with silver tissue and lace cuffs and a silver net hem. 23 inches. (Sotheby's)

Not all the lady modellers achieved the skills of these two famous ladies, but one may judge that there were ready customers for some of the coloured wax sheets marketed for various modelling pursuits. In 1844, the brothers John and Horatio Mintorn published a tiny pocket book called *Handbook for Modelling Flowers in Wax* dealing with wax flower modelling, an art that had apparently been perfected by their father. They commented on the special advantages of portraying flowers in three dimensions with shapes and colour that lasted. At a stall in the Pantheon Bazaar in London all the requisites of their wax art could be bought including paper patterns, paints and especially prepared sheets of coloured wax. It seems as though these sheets were reinforced with fabric, since they were shiny on one side and dull on the other and were also made in varying thicknesses. A steel curling pin 5 inches in length with a globular glass head was provided for shaping petals and picking up the fragments without over-handling. The colours were all warranted permanent and the "grain" ran with the length of the wax. The ingredients were said to be harmless, and scissors could be warmed by "placing in the mouth for a few moments."

At the same stall, where 12 sheets of coloured wax called Mintorn Art Fabric could be bought for one shilling, it was also possible to buy alabaster vases from Italy suitable for wax flower arrangements, fibrous leaves made from linen and glass "shades" or domes to protect the finished work. The stall was ideal for the finnicky handicraft of the period and no doubt was well patronized by the makers of fancy goods for bazaars, pedlar dolls and the miniature dolls boxed with a flowery bocage. Numbers of encased memorial or souvenir dolls were created in the Victorian period and accompanied by mock flower and foliage groups, bouquets or wreaths. Death was commonplace, infant mortality very high, and many a wax-doll was "laid to rest" at the same time as its little owner. Dolls were put into mourning when Prince Albert died. Osborne, the holiday home of the royal family, was said to seem like Pompeii, all life suddenly extinguished. Since white and violet were the only colours allowed, white wax flowers on black velvet became very fashionable for memorial caskets.

The Mintorn brothers were helped by their sister Mrs Mogridge and later in the century became very famous for their museum exhibits, in which wax flowers formed the background for stuffed birds and animals and for reproducing rare botanical specimens. They worked for three years at the New York Natural History Museum. In their book they advised using Madras wax treated with Canadian balsam. Another trick was to use honey to retain the "down" (pulverised blotting paper) on leaves, and arrowroot powder to reproduce the bloom on fruit such as peaches.

It is interesting to find that the Mintorns' little book was dedicated in very sycophantic terms to Her Grace the Duchess of Northumberland, with due deference to her "encouraging patronage." In 1831 Charlotte Florentia, Duchess of Northumberland, was appointed State Governess to the little Princess Victoria, who became queen six years later. Perhaps Victoria tried her hand at making wax flowers. She was 12 years old in 1831, and a little time before the famous artist William Behnes (1794-1864) had done a splendid bust of her in wax. It is a speaking likeness down to the slightly prominent front teeth. Behnes was appointed Sculptor in Ordinary to the Queen in 1837, and she herself had no small influence on Victorian doll-making, as we can judge (see page 66).

Below Three examples from the Powell Collection. Left: woollen dress trimmed with tiny buttons. 1883. 12 inches. Centre: small poured wax doll in an aesthetic costume with peacock feathers. 1881. 12 inches. Right: German-type wax doll in woollen suit, straw hat and leather boots. 1892. 11 inches. (Bethnal Green Museum of Childhood)

Below Three items from the Powell Collection. Left: wax-over composition lady in mourning for Queen Victoria. 1901. 12 inches. Centre: German character wax of a lady in court costume with a silk parasol and a fine outfit with a simulated feather boa over a silk dress with white gauze satin sash. 1901. 12 inches. Right: wax head doll dressed as a tennis-player in a navy-blue gown with a wide red sash and standing collar, a floppy brimmed hat and a little racquet. 1880. 12 inches. (Bethnal Green Museum of Childhood)

Gradually the popularity of waxworks began to wane, and they were replaced by mechanical museums. Madame Tussaud (see page 51) died in 1850 aged 90, but her premises survive to the present day and still present what the *Daily Telegraph* called her "ceroplastic panorama of the men of the day." Interest in other countries and their peoples promoted some important waxworks in Victorian times: the Oriental and Turkish Museum in Knightsbridge opened in 1854 and displayed some fine figures modelled by James Boggi from Eastern life, including costume, arms and implements, set scenes of Turkish baths, coffee shops and bazaars, a wedding and street scenes. It is amusing to find that almost at the same moment an English lady in a true Turkish harem was teaching some of the seductive ladies to dress dolls (see page 104)! John Timbs, writing in the *Curiosities of London* (1868), also extolled the work of one Napoleon Montanari (see page 86) who won a medal in the Great Exhibition of 1851. His models were shown at the Linwood Gallery in Leicester Square and were "life-like and spirited figures of costumed natives of Mexico and American Indians, modelled in wax with surprising minuteness and artistic feeling both in the position and grouping, varied expression and anatomical development" (see page 91).

Although the Mintorn brothers became famous chiefly because their art coincided with the discovery and arrival in Britain of many new botanical rarities, wax flower-modelling was not a new art. It probably originated among convent nuns in Italy, who in the Middle Ages made garlands to decorate their plaster figures of saints and the Virgin Mary; these were also in demand for placing on graves. Princess Mary of Modena, who in 1673 married James II of England as his second wife, is known to have introduced the craft to the English court. The Earl of Peterborough, who had searched for a bride for the king, described her as "a young creature about Fourteen years of Age who carried such a Light of Beauty, such Characters of Ingenuity and Goodness as surprised the eyes." She was in fact a mere girl of fifteen and she came to court to find she had step-daughters of eleven and seven. Wax work became very popular and in 1686 Lady Margaret Russell described the fine models of fruit and flowers in her private chapel as the work of nuns.

It will be suspected that I am diverging far from the topic of wax dolls, but it is fascinating to discover a certain link between Mary of Modena and two quite outstanding early wax dolls that must have been brought to England in 1673. When the famous collection of dolls which included the 17th-century wooden dolls "Lord and Lady Clapham" was sold at Sotheby's, London, in 1974, these two wax dolls were sold as well. The collection originally passed down through the Cockerell family, who were related to Samuel Pepys. But the wax dolls belonged to a Miss Bivar, one of three sisters who came to England with Mary of Modena. Miss Bivar married a Mr Billi, who became a naturalized Englishman. Their grandson, John Billi, married Elizabeth Cockerell and from their daughter Mary Frances the whole collection passed down the female line to the present day. Were the dolls also made in a nunnery and then dressed in their fashionable clothes? They seem to be cast in an identical mould and are beautifully modelled. The heads and hands of poured wax are sewn to the fabric-stuffed body, they measure 23 inches and both have brown glass eyes. One still has the remnants of a wig of dark hair (see pages 31 and 35).

The modern doll-collector may find so much history tedious. But in questioning why in the 19th century the rather unlikely phenomenon of wax dolls for children arose, I found the contributory causes reaching further and further back. It was necessary to touch on the mysticism of wax and its importance to the Christian Church, since modelling often had religious motives. From the technical point of view, it was especially important to trace the methods used by the makers of early portrait figures, since they initiated the use of hair, eyes, clothes and ornaments for realism. The setting up of popular waxwork shows enabled a number of people to be apprenticed in the art of making such models, and some of these eventually branched out as toy-makers, probably when waxwork shows were losing popularity and they needed a new livelihood.

Certainly, by about the end of the 18th century the quality of the carved and turned wooden doll, originally so carefully and beautifully made, had deteriorated. On the whole, such dolls had been an expensive toy for aristocratic children, beautifully costumed in period dress. Not only were such dolls considered old-fashioned in 1800, but a more realistic "baby" was being demanded, one that, since it was available to a larger public, could be produced more cheaply and easily. For speed of construction a *papier-mâché* moulded mask or head could be used, and a wax covering complexion provided an agreeable asset. Who initiated the first dolls of this kind is not known, but no doubt they quickly became a popular novelty and were rapidly imitated. Wax-modellers, experienced in the art of modelling infants and small children, would easily conceive the idea of producing miniature children, even miniature "Royal Children" in imitation of Victoria's little princes and princesses. The eventual product of the wax-modeller turned doll-maker was a poured wax head and limbs added to a soft fabric stuffed body.

In the next chapters (in roughly chronological order) I have detailed some of the characteristics of individual makers (and schools or families of makers) and have included such personal history as I have been able to discover from public records or the accounts of descendants. Often it is impossible to generalize since the doll-makers' work varied over a period of time, both in the materials they used and the moulds they designed. Nevertheless, I hope that this information will give some guidance in identifying these very interesting antique dolls.

By the end of the 19th century, other methods of doll-making were established, and fine-quality bisque creations had superseded the old-fashioned wax doll. The last of the wax doll-makers had to use their skills in a variety of ways, by making tailors' dummies or coiffeur heads for hair-dressers in order to earn a living. Only now, in modern times, has there been some sort of renaissance of wax doll-making. It is no longer for children, however, but is a partnership established between collectors and skilled wax-modellers who can restore antiques or emulate the work of the past by making new models in the old style.

Early Records of Doll-Makers

Above Portrait of three young sisters, the youngest holding a period doll. Attributed to the English School of Robert Peake. C.1620. (Sotheby's)

Right Fashion doll in court costume with a compass hanging at the waist. A silver wire supports the frontage, and there is breast decor and a wired skirt. French, C.1760. 9 inches. (Museum of London)

Opposite Two dolls from the Powell Collection. Left: wax head and arms, pink, lime and green striped dress trimmed with lace and furbelows for a 16-year-old lady, and a white lace cap. 1758. 11 inches. Right: wax head and limbs on a fabric body with red moulded wax shoes and striped brocaded silk dress. 1757. 8 inches. (Bethnal Green Museum of Childhood)

For examples of very early dolls one often has to rely on literary records, and even then it may not be clear what material the doll was made of. To see some of the earliest surviving wax dolls we have to visit their own homes: the priceless dolls' houses still inhabited by little dressed wax dolls which cunningly represent the characters of the times in which they lived. The group on page 42 from the Rijksmuseum in Amsterdam shows a family from the last quarter of the 17th century. The waxwork is exquisite but tiny, and the clothing itself is obviously what makes the dolls important. The sumptuous dolls' house is housed in a cabinet divided into rooms and furnished with every detail of 17th-century Dutch life and is considered to be work carried out in Amsterdam.

The mania for rich collecting cabinets first became established in the 16th century. At that time Augsburg and Ulm in Germany were famous for dolls' houses and their fittings, and it was said that the miniatures required were all made by specialist craftsmen. (The Guild system stopped the development of toy factories as it prohibited a man practising other than his own trade.) In 1698, Christopher Weigel commented that collecting had given a great fillip to trade, and that some things were made by gold- and

silver-smiths, some by wood-turners, some by carvers in alabaster, and that others were "moulded out of wax, and in particular many kinds of beasts and fowls are made of this almost exactly like nature, with their rough skins drawn over them or very prettily bedecked with feathers." So the wax dolls were able to enjoy both gardens and farmyards.

Generally the fine wax dolls made in the 17th and 18th centuries must have been intended as luxury presents for some child of high rank or as a fashionable curiosity for a noble lady. Yet we must conclude that some of them were intended for play. During 1716, the famous Lady Mary Wortley Montagu, on her way to reside in Turkey, stayed in Vienna. The party was invited to visit the collection of the Prince of Lichtenstein, who had died in 1712. This included marvellous jewellery and automata, but among the cabinets of curiosities collected as the Prince's "Treasure" Lady Mary discovered some dolls: "The next Cabinet diverted me yet better, being nothing else but a parcel of wax babys and Toys in ivory, very well worthy to be presented to children of five years old." The last comment is surprising for the period, but as her small son was travelling with the party possibly her thoughts were with him.

Even more luxurious was the doll described by Daniel Defoe, who reported in the *Daily Post* in 1725 from Paris that:

> The Duchess of Orleans made a present to the Infant Queen of a wax baby three foot high with diamond earrings, a necklace of pearls and diamond cross, with a Furniture of plate for a toilet, and two Indian Chests full of linen and several suits of cloaths for the baby, the whole for the Princess to play with.

Since at that time Paris led the fashion world, wax dolls were used to carry abroad the vogues in dress and coiffeur. In many cases they were no more than little wax mannequins and were sometimes made with a stiff

Right 18th-century wax head and arms fashion doll in French court dress from the time of Louis XV. The darkened solid wax head sits on a wire coming from the torso, there is a linen-wrapped armature body to the waist, a cone of moulded cardboard from the waist down, there are no legs, and the doll is wired to a wooden stand. The doll has bead eyes, the wig has gone, and there are no ears. The costume is tattered but quite wonderful. The silk-lined outer dress is of pink and white striped silk with scattered bunches of pink roses and green leaves. The hem is a 1½-inch gold metallic fringe, and a pleated ribbon trim with finished edges runs down the front of the bodice and to the sides of the sizeable back train. The dress is pinned to the body with many tiny pins. 9½ inches. (From the Mrs Nevill Jackson Collection, England, through the Eleanor Cole Coolidge Collection to the Wenham Museum, Massachussetts)

stand to hold them erect rather than legs, which in any case would not show beneath deep skirts. They were probably quite expensive. A German newspaper of 1689 lampooned them with these words: "Not only do our women folk themselves travel to France, but they pay as many thalers for their models: these dressed up dolls to be sent to them, as would serve to emulate the very frippery of the devil."

So these little travellers reached London and Berlin and some went even further afield to America where the *New England Weekly Journal* carried an advertisement in 1733 that a mannequin in the latest fashion was on display in Boston. By the second half of the 18th century London was setting its own fashions and in 1751 an announcement appeared in the *Gentleman's Magazine* that "several mannequins with different styles of dress made in St James' Street in order to give Tsarina Elizabeth an idea of

Opposite Wax portrait doll of Madame Tussaud. (Museum of London)

Right "Tussaud" Caroline Harris baby doll with wax arms, fabric body and legs. ?1798. 24 inches. (Mrs Betty Simson)

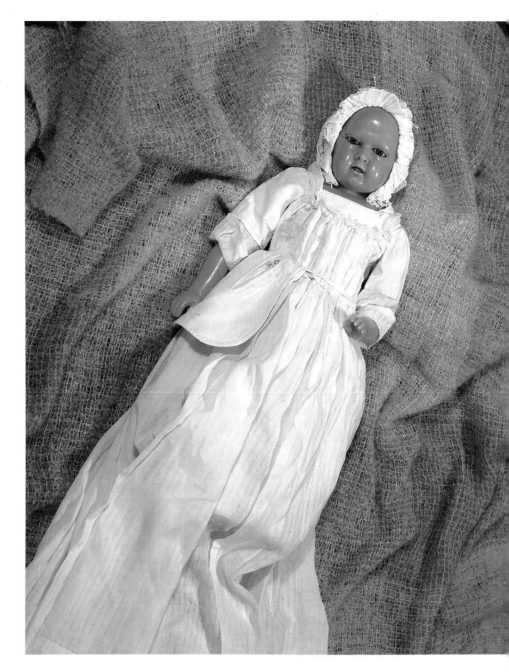

Right Early 19th-century mechanical novelty wax-headed nurse and baby. The head and torso of the nurse seem to be of a tan-coloured composition of some sort with a wax mask forming the face. Perhaps originally the entire head was waxed but the back portion has now vanished. The remains of the hair suggest that it was perhaps tow from flax. The eyes are black bead, and the mouth and brows are painted. The lower torso and legs of crude wood are mounted on an unpainted wood platform, 2¾ inches square. The wire arms are connected to string which extends from a hole in the platform bottom. When the string is pulled, the nurse lifts her basket of vegetables and the baby, which she holds in her left hand. The baby's wax mask face and hair are moulded over a 2¾-inch wood stick, from which a moulded counter-weight ball hangs by a string. The clothing is totally original on both dolls, and reveals careful mending on the baby's dress. The fabrics are hand-woven linen – coarser on the nurse, finer on the baby. Both have a fringed trim on the hem, and nurse has the remains of a ribbon cap, baby a ribbon frill around its face. The nurse's petticoat is coarse paper and she has no underclothes. 8 inches. (From the Mrs Nevill Jackson Collection to the Wenham Museum, Massachussetts)

Opposite Wax doll in wedding dress. 1761. 12 inches. (Powell Collection, Bethnal Green Museum of Childhood)

fashion dressing have been despatched to Russia." We can assume that many of them were made of wax since it was both in fashion and most delicate for portraiture. Some of the wax dolls that survive from this period are very fashionably dressed, and even when they have a history of belonging to some child it is not clear if that was in fact their original purpose.

At least we are left in no doubt that the dolls in the Powell Collection are "fashion" dolls. Few dolls come down the ages so well documented, since this famous miniature mannequin parade, now in the Bethnal Green

Museum, London, is a series of 44 dolls dressed by members of one family between 1754 and 1910. They were given costumes to illustrate the fashion of the year in which they were dressed, and they also provide an interesting dated catalogue of doll production. A good number of them are wax, or wax over *papier-mâché* or composition. They are mostly small, cheap dolls, none much larger than 12 inches, and we would give a great deal to know at what shop or bazaar they were bought over the years.

The procession is headed by a little 8 inch wax doll, now legless, dressed by Laetitia Clark in 1754 when she was 12 years old. Seven years and seven dolls later she married David Powell, a London merchant, at St Botolph's Church, Bishopsgate and a doll was dressed in scraps of the bride's dress. "Mrs Powell's Wedding suite 1761" reads the proud label (see page 47). She wears silk brocade trimmed with lace with a lace pelerine with lace cap and a bead necklace. The original maker had four sons, one of whom, James, married Catherine Cotton, who carried on the family tradition. It was Catherine's grandson and granddaughters who treasured the collection and eventually saw it installed in the Victoria and Albert Museum for posterity to admire. The later dolls in the collection were dressed by their mother. There are big gaps in the date sequence, maybe because some dolls were lost, but what a happy idea for a family to pursue and what an historic treasure! The Powell family celebrated by these dolls also became very famous through Laetitia's great grandson: General Sir Robert Baden Powell, hero of Mafeking and founder of the Boy Scout movement.

Catherine Andras

Catherine Andras (1775-1860) was an orphan who lived with her three sisters in Bristol where they ran a toy and perfumery business. While very young she modelled wax dolls as a consignment for a fair, and from that she progressed to modelling "likenesses". When John Wesley came to Bristol in 1790, at the age of 87, she modelled him from life. Later Catherine was adopted in London by the miniaturist Robert Bowyer, who had lost his own daughter. He opened an Historical Gallery over his house at 87, Pall Mall, enlisting such famous artists as Benjamin West, Philippe Jacques de Loutherbourg and Robert Smirke to contribute to a sumptuous *History of England* in paintings.

Catherine's models were of coloured wax and most elaborately finished, with eyelashes and eyebrows of the finest hair and fur obtainable. Her portraits were exhibited at the Royal Academy from 1799 to 1824. During this time she was appointed Modeller in Wax to Queen Charlotte and was awarded the "Larger Silver Pallet" by the Society for the Encouragement of the Arts, Manufactures and Commerce for her models of Princess Charlotte and Lord Nelson. She worked at the Historical Gallery, and the little princess was brought to her there in 1801 when the child was five. Her first model of Nelson was done during his lifetime, and Lady Hamilton considered the full-sized wax effigy made after his death and furnished with his own uniform to be the finest likeness ever made. Catherine, who was paid £104 14 shillings and 9 pence, used the shoe buckles Nelson was wearing when he was killed and his hat with the small piece of green cloth that sheltered his remaining eye from the sun. The figure is now in Westminster Abbey.

Sadly, no example of a doll made by Catherine Andras has come to light. The Historical Gallery was a failure and was eventually dispersed at an expensive lottery. Prizes included original paintings and also sets of the engraved *History of England*.

Madame Tussaud

It is difficult to know whether Madame Tussaud (1761-1850) should be included among the doll-makers, since it is not certain that she ever designed an actual doll. Her famous waxwork show, which has lasted from the late 18th century to the present day, has led people to attribute her name to family treasures and to wax models with an uncertain history which have found their way into museum collections.

Modern research (see the book *Marie Tussaud* by Leslie and Chapman, 1978) seems to pose a few interesting questions on her birth and early life. For some reason, Madame Tussaud herself claimed that she was born in Berne, Switzerland, when in fact her baptismal certificate proves that she was born in Strasbourg. Her mother was only 18 and had been baptized Anna Maria Walder in the same church as her daughter, St Peter's. The baby was christened Anna Marie Grosholtz and her father was said to have been a soldier on the staff of General Würmser who had died of wounds two months before the birth of his little daughter. Curiously, there is no documentary evidence of the marriage. However, it has always been stated that Marie was adopted by her maternal uncle, the famous Parisian wax modeller Philippe Guillaume Mathé Curtius, but it would seem that he was only Marie's "adopted" uncle and not, as is often stated, her mother's brother.

Curtius had acquired medical qualifications when quite a young man and, as was often the method in that period, he used moulded wax replicas of anatomical organs to demonstrate his research, becoming very skilled in their manufacture. From modelling he turned to portraiture and in 1757 set up a small museum in Berne. It was here in fact that the widowed Madame Grosholtz came to keep house for him and brought with her the two-year old Marie. Was there a closer relationship between master and maid? He was 26 and she was 20. It has been hinted that he was more than an uncle and tutor to the clever little girl who became Marie Tussaud. She inherited his skills and eventually also became his heir. Certainly after he had removed to Paris and established his famous *Cabinet de Cire* (wax works), he officially adopted the child and all of them lived together.

The *Cabinet de Cire* proved a successful and fashionable venture, and as she grew up Marie was able to meet numerous famous people, many of whom wished for a wax portrait. The method used was similar to taking a "death mask." A plaster cast was taken of the subject, who had to submit to the rather uncomfortable process of having his face oiled and quills inserted in his nostrils to permit breathing.

Marie grew very proficient in the arts of modelling, finishing sculpture, hair insertion and all the arts of the studio. When the king's young sister Elisabeth visited the waxworks, she was so attracted by Marie and enthusiastic about her work that the royal family allowed her to invite Marie to Versailles to instruct her. When Marie took up this invitation in 1780, she was 18 and Elisabeth 14. She taught her young pupil how to model fruit and flowers in wax and also, since she was a devout Roman

Below English wax-over doll with moving tongue and eyes worked by wire pull in crutch. C.1820, redressed in 1845. 25 inches. (Bethnal Green Museum of Childhood)

Opposite This English wax-over *papier-mâché* doll is said to have belonged originally to the eldest daughter of Queen Victoria, Vicky, or "Pussy" as the royal family called the favourite child. She was born in 1840, and the doll probably dates from between 1845 and 1850. She has sleeping eyes worked by a wire at the left wrist and is so carefully modelled that her toe and finger nails are delinated. Her pretty ringlets of real hair are on a stitched base. The dress is of a well-preserved shot silk, striped taffeta type, also V-yoke style. Compare the tooled mouth with the Bloomer doll of similar make. 19 inches. (Tunbridge Wells Museum)

Above Close-up view of Caroline Harris baby doll. 24 inches. (Mrs Simson)

Catholic, little votive arms and legs and religious figures. The two girls became friends and companions, but in 1789 the deteriorating political situation led Curtius to call Marie home. The tragic incidents of the French Revolution are well known, and to Marie fell some of the gruesome tasks of modelling heads that had actually been guillotined. Her friend was executed together with the rest of the royal family.

After her uncle died in 1794, Marie married Monsieur Tussaud, about whom very little is known, though it is thought that he toured England with Curtius' *Grand Cabinet of Curiosities*, as it was called in English, in 1795. During the next five years they had three children. The first, a girl, Marie Marguerite Pauline, who was born in September 1796, only lived six months, but it is recorded that Madame Tussaud made a model of her baby. Her son Joseph was born in 1798 and the younger son Francis in 1800. For some reason, probably economic, the adventurous little woman obtained permission to take her waxworks to show in England and, taking Joseph with her, she set off in 1802, leaving Francis with her husband and mother in Paris. From the letters which survive, she must have had a very hard struggle before she became famous. She travelled the length and breadth of the British Isles, showing in major towns everywhere and finally establishing her exhibition permanently in London. Her memoirs gave no clue as to why she never returned to Paris and her husband. Francis joined them in London when he was 21, and Marie herself lived to be nearly 90, a wonderful old lady, able to the end to entertain visitors with astonishing recollections of the past.

The major part of Madame Tussaud's original and priceless collection was destroyed in a disastrous fire in 1925, but it is intriguing to find that privately owned examples of her work may survive: a claim made for both the "babies" illustrated left and opposite. It is known that Marie did undertake work on private commissions. When she was showing her exhibition in Glasgow in October 1803, she advertised in the *Glasgow Herald*: "Mme. Tussaud offers to take portraits in the fullest imitation of life," adding, "The artist can also model from the dead body as well as from animated nature." She showed a portrait of herself and her infant daughter Marie. (The portrait wax in the Museum of London that purports to be Madame Tussaud when young certainly has a strong likeness to the lithograph by F. Hervé included in her memoirs, but its origin is unknown.)

Marie's fame must soon have spread, for she received a royal commission in 1803 when the Duchess of York (married to the second son of George III) asked her to make a model of a sleeping baby for her. This she carried out, keeping a model for her own exhibition. She must, one feels sure, have known some of the French aristocrats who had fled from the Terror in the Revolution years, and perhaps they gave her useful introductions. She showed many souvenirs of the ill-fated French royal family, including a group of Louis XVI and Marie Antoinette with their son, aged about five "represented in the dress he usually wore." She also modelled the Dauphin, the older son Louis Joseph, and was distressed when he died in 1789 as an infant. The Nantucket Historical Association of USA owns a model baby, a life-sized wax with brown eyes said to have been modelled from the Dauphin by Marie Tussaud. According to a letter of 1852, it was brought back as a present to one Priscilla Coffin in 1796 by

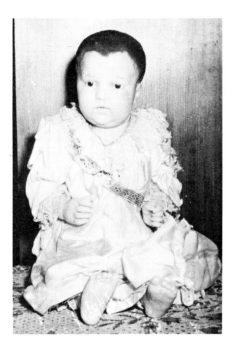

Above Life-size Little Dauphin model. 1796.
(Nantucket Historical Association)

her father, a sea captain. The workmanship is outstanding and of the period, but there is no proof to connect it with Curtius or with Tussaud.

Family history definitely attributes the doll shown on page 00 to Madame Tussaud. She is said to represent Caroline Harris, born on November 22, 1798. The tradition has been passed on by word of mouth among the family to whom the doll still belongs. Caroline married at the age of 37 and died in her 76th year. An unmarried sister, Lydia, then inherited the doll and in turn passed it on to a niece. The Harris family were Quakers living in Walthamstow, and Caroline's father was a corn factor, said to have had some dealings with France. Could the family have had some personal connection with Madame Tussaud? The date presents a difficulty since in 1798 Madame Tussaud herself had a baby and was in Paris, and only came to England much later, when Caroline Harris was almost four years old.

This fine wax doll measures 24 inches from top to toe, though the actual head and bust of wax are only 6¼ inches, being mounted on a stuffed body and legs with rather simply moulded "doll" arms of wax. There is no attempt to "prettify" the features, which could well be a likeness of a specific baby. She has very beautiful, fine quality "paper-weight" blue eyes with a black pupil. The eyes were made to close by a wire (now missing) that came from the crutch. The bald head seems to represent a very young infant, but there are three small brass pins showing, one beneath each ear and one on top of the crown, which must have pinned on a bonnet or wig. The mouth is interesting as it is slightly open to reveal the tongue and bare gums. In the upper gum, two deep indents either represent the marks for milk teeth or actual sockets which once held little teeth. The chubby baby is dressed in the original clothes of Caroline Harris: a gown and linen "pocket" with handkerchief confirmed by experts as late 18th century. The outstanding fact must be that this was designed as a play doll (and was certainly played with – the hands are worn at the finger tips); it is a very early, surviving baby model doll made in the finest tradition of poured wax skill. It seems to be a unique example and one would love to be able to prove that it was the work of the famous Madame Tussaud, and to learn how that came to pass.

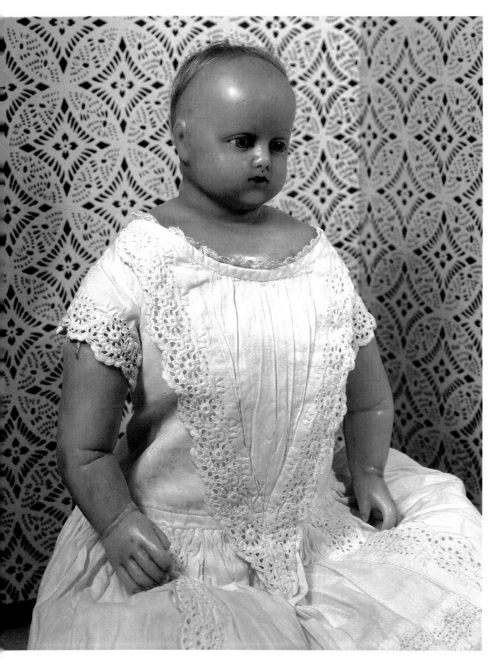

Opposite Model of Queen Victoria in coronation robes and crown. Kid body mounted on a wooden frame with simulated little slippered feet. *C.*1840. 23½ inches. (Bethnal Green Museum of Childhood)

Above Royal model wax doll, made by Pierotti, probably in 1841. 19 inches. (Mrs Heather Bond)

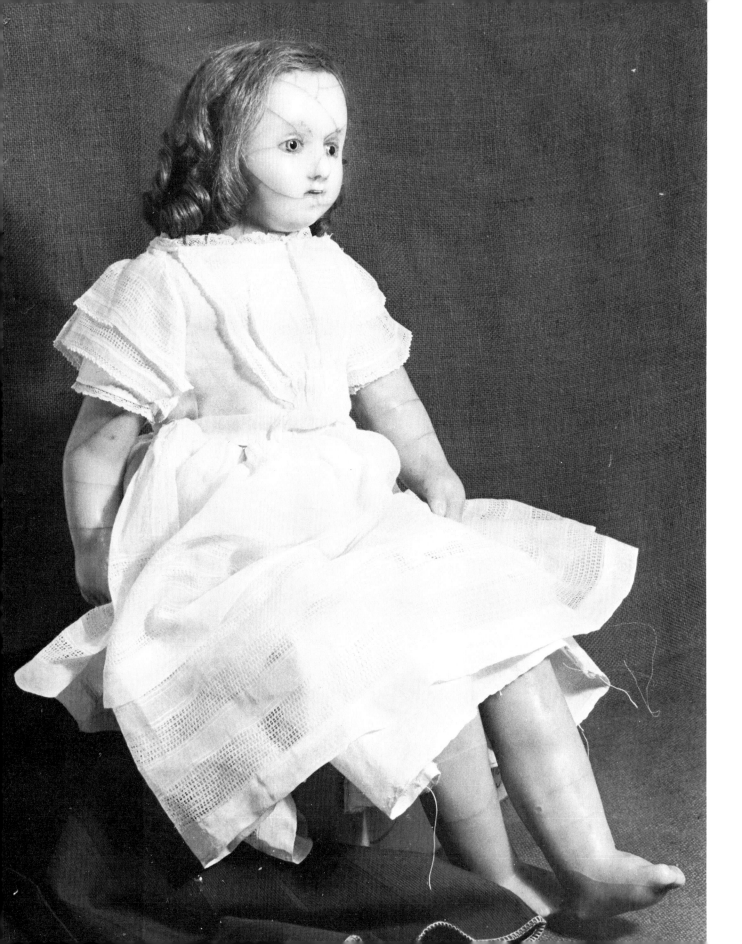

Early Doll-Making in London

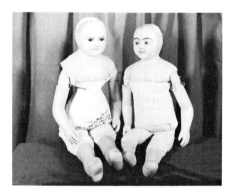

Above Large English wax over *papier-mâché* dolls showing their body construction. (Wenham Museum, Massachusetts)

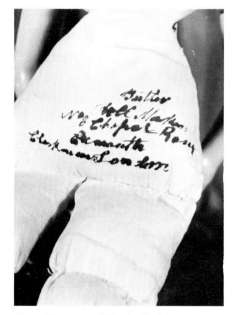

Above Signature of Charles Butler. (Wenham Museum, Massachusetts)

Opposite Fine-quality wax over *papier-mâché* English doll. Like the Santy doll "Rosa Mary" (see page 48), it has rather thick arms and well defined feet and hands. This child-like doll was popular in the first half of the 19th century. C.1840. 26 inches. (Somerset County Museum, Taunton)

The first quarter of the 19th century saw one of those odd changes in doll fashions that illustrate a period of social history. In England the Industrial Revolution was reducing some craft-workers to penury and promoting mechanically-minded businessmen to fortune. It turned society topsy-turvy, brought many seeking work to the towns and began to establish a prosperous middle class. This may not seem to have a lot of relevance to dolls, but, whereas until the turn of the century it had been mainly very wealthy families who bought expensive dolls for their children, the trade now began to expand and demand was far greater.

Wooden dolls had become less popular and cruder. One famous maker commented sadly on the decline in his art, remarking that, while dolls were once well carved, now scarcely a nose was indicated – "nothing to call a nose," he said. Wooden dolls were superseded by much more naturalistic wax over *papier-mâché* dolls, and there were several important doll-makers working east of the centre of London in Clerkenwell and Shoreditch.

In 1850 Henry Mayhew wrote in his survey of *London Labour and the London Poor* that:

> The manufacture of dolls employs many hands, being divided into many distinct branches. The two main divisions are the "WOODEN" and "SEWED" dolls. The former being the dolls of the poor and the latter those of the rich. The wooden dolls are exceedingly primitive in their structure, there is no attempt at symmetry in the body, whilst the limbs are mere slips of lath joined. The sewed dolls rank much higher as works of art. Whether this is the consequence of the cause of a greater division of labour it is difficult to say; suffice it that whereas the wooden doll is generally begun and completed by hand (with the exception of the wig) the sewed doll has as many distinct branches as it is divisible into distinct parts. In the first place there is the sewer and stuffer – the calico integuments being generally cut out by the manufacturer and given out with the sawdust, hair or wool with which the body is to be filled, to the same party. Then there is the doll's head maker and the doll dresser. Each of these are separate branches of the trade. Occasionally some family may be met with where the whole of the branches (with the exception of the making of the eyes) are performed; but this is far from usual especially with the better description of work.

In fact, the very different types of work needed the individual skills of both women and men, and often children in a poor family also helped. One of the men Mayhew questioned said it was starvation work. "Oh Sir, the children of the people who will be happy with my dolls little think

Opposite Fortune-telling gypsy doll made by Charles Pierotti for sale in a bazaar. The doll is brown tinted and is mounted on a wooden handle. When the doll was spun round, little gifts on her skirt were distributed to children. 23 inches. (Bethnal Green Museum of Childhood)

Above This doll has a curious and unique history, and since it does not resemble a known pattern of wax doll may have been made up by a local doll-maker. Perhaps it is a portrait doll as it does not conform to a model. In 1840 a little girl, Mary Anne Marriott, had her pretty golden red hair trimmed short after a serious illness. (In Victorian times long hair was sometimes considered debilitating.) To console her for the loss, a doll was made up and some of the lost tresses used for the doll hair. The poured shoulder head, legs and arms are stitched on to the fabric body. 16 inches. (Tunbridge Wells Museum)

under what circumstances they are made, nor do their parents – I wish they did." He made the composition heads of *papier-mâché*, or "paper mashed" as he called it, using a mould to shape the head in a peculiar kind of "sugar paper." (This coarse blue paper originally used for packing sugar loaf can be seen in early dolls.) Together he and his 15-year-old daughter could make 12 or 13 dozen a day of small heads and were paid four pence per dozen. On average he thought he scarcely made 15 shillings each week, and that was augmented by the small amounts his wife could earn stuffing leather arms. His *papier-mâché* heads went to the maker to be waxed and made into complete dolls, and no doubt another out-worker made their dresses.

The superior dolls had wigs of finely-curled human hair in ringlets, and this was another separate trade, as was the specialist manufacture of glass eyes. When Mayhew was making his survey in 1850 there were only two makers of glass eyes in London and the man he questioned was reluctant to give away any trade secrets. He said that he had been in the trade for 40 years and his father before him. They made all sorts of eyes both for human beings and for taxidermy as well as dolls. The cheapest type were mere small, hollow glass spheres made of white enamel and coloured either black or blue. The best quality, blown-glass dolls' eyes were made to look realistic, and to produce the desired colours it was necessary to be a good chemist and use the correct metallic oxides on the fire. Ordinary eyes cost five shillings for 12 dozen pairs, while good ones cost 4 pence per pair, and they took longer to make. He emphasized that many of the eyes were made for export and that a great number of dolls were sent to America.

> They can't make waxdolls in America Sir, owing to the climate. The wax won't set in very hot weather and it cracks in very cold. I know a party who went out there to start as a doll maker. He took several gross of my eyes with him but he couldn't make a success. The eyes we make for Spanish America are black. A blue-eyed doll in that country wouldn't sell at all. Here, however, nothing goes down but blue eyes. The reason for that is because that's the colour of the Queen's eyes and she sets the fashion in this as in other things.

This glass-eye maker said that the largest order he had ever received was from the "Speaking Doll Maker" in High Holborn and that was for £50. (See page 71.)

While on the topic of glass eyes one should mention that many of the large wax-over dolls (dolls with a *papier-mâché* head coated in wax over painted features and painted or glass eyes) of the first half of 19th century have curious dark grey eyes. In the best dolls a wire pull was run through their body to close their eyes and make them seem asleep. Later in the century one of the most famous glass eye makers was Charles Pache & Son of Lower Hurst Street, Birmingham. Pache saw an exhibit of artificial eyes made in France at the Great Exhibition in 1851 and thought he could achieve similar results at his own glass works. The firm, which lasted for three generations until 1914, produced fine glass eyes as an important part of their trade. In 1876, when George Bartley was writing about John Edwards' factory (see pages 133-5), he said that English-made eyes were only used for the very finest dolls and models for exhibition. For cheaper dolls, hundreds of eyes in assorted sizes were imported from Germany.

The newly popular production of fine dolls in the early years of the 19th century brought of course the opening of shops where they could be bought. Most doll-makers assembled the dolls in home premises, and they then had to be brought either to a shop or to a warehouse to be sold wholesale. The very cheapest were often hawked around the streets in a basket or from a little street booth. Popular parades were held in Regent's Park and Hyde Park, and there was the certainty of well-to-do children enjoying an outing with their parents or nanny. "Spoiled children are our best customers," said one poor woman earning her living in this way. "If we hear a young miss say she *will* have one and cries for it we are sure of a good price." The poor women who trudged around with these penny dolls lived off Leather Lane and Somers Town and stocked up at a dealer in Houndsditch such as Alfred Davis or White's. The living was a poor one but occasionally an ambitious person might better themself. Mayhew interviewed one "Dick the Doll Man" who thought he was the first to call "Dolls three a Shilling" – hawkers customarily called their wares out loud. Later he married a girl whom he had met selling dolls from a basket and, having paid a guinea to learn doll-making, he went on to model wax figures and large-size heads for show-men. Eventually he joined a travelling showman, Biancis, as doorman and also pursued the doll trade with his wife.

The best dolls could be bought at luxury shops in London. During the 18th century shops are recorded with such picturesque names as The Noah's Ark (founded in 1760 by the Cornishman William Hamley and now continued at 200 Regent's Street under the same name but not the same family), The Three Rabbits and The Orange Tree. Charles Dickens described a toyshop sign which showed "a tight fat little Harlequin who rode a rocking horse." These shops sold a mixture of luxury goods, no doubt including dolls. Milliners also probably used dolls as a useful adjunct to their stock and for display purposes. One such was certainly Mrs C.E. Brown of 13/14 New Bond Street, London. A wax-covered doll in the collection of the Bethnal Green Museum of Childhood has two pretty straw hats, one of which, lavishly trimmed with a dark green feather, bears a tiny miniature copper-plate trade label. The label advertises this ladies' shop as founded in 1829 and announces Mrs Brown as Warrant-Holder to Her Majesty. Obviously this doll must date from after Victoria's coronation in 1837, and the Lion and Unicorn crest is playfully done as though for a nursery audience.

But though the aristocracy and the fashionable world of Bond Street may have patronized such shops, the world and his wife thronged the popular bazaars that sprang up in London in the early 19th century. There were the Pantheon Bazaar and the Royal Bazaar (renamed Queen's Bazaar when it was rebuilt after a fire in 1829) in Oxford Street. The word bazaar was borrowed from the Turkish and stood for a conglomerate of goods ranged together for sale, and these places did offer retail stalls with what a contemporary newspaper called "bijouterie and nic-nacs." Best of all, they staged all sorts of exhibitions of art and sculpture, waxworks, paper-work crafts and even the new-found science of photography and magic-lantern. Everything was done to entice the public inside, and they became fashionable meeting-places and useful markets. At the Pantheon, Mintorn sold his wax supplies and Pierotti his dolls (see pages 34 and 78).

Right Hand-sculpted model of General Roberts made by Charles Pierotti during the Boer War, when Roberts was Commander-in-Chief of the British Army. Wax head, arms, legs and inset hair, moustache and eyebrows. The expression is keen and lifelike. Miniature medals are simulated by toy metal coins of the realm. 1901. 19 inches. (Bethnal Green Museum of Childhood)

Opposite Wax portrait doll of King Edward VII at time of his coronation in 1901. The hair is very realistically set with a mixture of blond and grey hairs to achieve a greying effect; the moustache, beard and eyebrows have been treated similarly; the centre crown has been left bald. Pierotti work. 21 inches. (Museum of London)

Most of these fashionable bazaars were organized for profit, and in some cases their owners made a fortune from rents and fees. The Soho Bazaar on the edge of Oxford Street was rather different, being planned originally with a benevolent motive. It stood at numbers 4, 5 and 6 Soho Square and was first opened in 1816. The Napoleonic Wars in Europe left many widows and orphans, dependents of soldiers killed abroad, and brought much unemployment and poverty. A Mr John Trotter suggested that a government-run establishment could provide a respectable livelihood for people with a low income. He offered his empty premises in Soho Square free of expense for several years, agreeing to organize the scheme and run it himself, not for profit. As the government would not agree, he went ahead with his philanthropic ideal on his own, opened the place on

Above Engraving from a painting by Landseer, 1842, of Queen Victoria with the Princess Royal and the Prince of Wales. (Mary Hillier)

Above Doll in pram, representing Princess Beatrice. The doll belonged to a family that originally owned dolls of all the royal children. (Private collection)

February 1, 1816 and it flourished. This was mainly so because he limited the stall-holders to efficient and trustworthy people, who had to produce a signed testimonial. The stalls mostly sold fancy goods. Dolls made by Madame Montanari and by the firm of Marsh are found with the Soho Bazaar address. Numbers referred to a stall holding. For example: "Santy, inventor, 340 Long Room, Soho Bazaar," or "Chas Marsh 31, 32 Corinthian Bazaar."

A little later another famous toy bazaar was opened in the Lowther Arcade, a curved and roofed-over avenue that connected the Strand and Adelaide Street. The 245-feet-long Arcade was designed by Witheron Young in 1830-2 and was full of small shops. As they dealt in the popular end of the market, much of their stock would have been cheap European toys and dolls. Luxury wax dolls made by Marsh, Pierotti and Edwards were stocked by famous shops such as Peacock's "The Beaming Nurse" or Morrell's (see page 82). At the end of the century Hamley's in Regent Street were stocking Pierotti and Mrs Lucy Peck was using the Montanari work (see page 140).

So much for the London commercial scene. The really important influence on English wax dolls occurred in the 1840s. There is an illuminating sentence in Julie Maitland's little book published in 1850, *The Doll and her Friends: Memoirs of Lady Seraphina*:

> I am but a small doll, not one of those splendid specimens of wax modelled from the Princess Royal with distinct fingers and toes, eyes that shut and tongues that wag. I first opened my eyes to the light of the Pantheon Bazaar – a silver paper covering was removed from my face and the world burst into my view.

It is clear from this that royal model dolls were both a sensation and an expensive fashionable toy. After considering all the likely contenders, I feel sure that it was the Pierotti family who inaugurated this type of doll, and they obviously enjoyed a very popular success.

When the young Queen Victoria married her cousin Albert of Saxe-Cobourg-Gotha in 1840, the match was not popular with her subjects, and the fact that they proceeded to produce a large family of children in rather quick succession was also criticized. A cheeky cartoon of April 25, 1843 headed *Tender Annuals* showed Prince Albert as a gardener with two small children in glass forcing-frames and about to transfer a small baby from a flowerpot. John Bull, watching, cries "Hollo, hollo young man come come! I shall have such a stock o' them sort of plants on my hands, I shan't know what to do with them!" A row of little pots numbered 1844-51 echoed the nation's fears of an annual addition to the royal family and the consequent drain on the taxpayers' purse. There were in fact nine royal children by 1857, despite the fact that Queen Victoria always professed herself disenchanted with the role of motherhood. The eldest child, the Princess Royal, Victoria, or "Vicky" or "Pussy" as her family called her, was born in 1840; Edward, Prince of Wales, in 1841; Alice in 1843; Alfred in 1844; Helena in 1846; Louise in 1848; Arthur in 1850; Leopold in 1853 and Beatrice in 1857.

Then as now royal babies were of great interest to the public, and the Queen and her escort became increasingly popular with the prosperity and success of their reign. It is interesting to remember also that the period

Above George W. Tuttle's doll exhibit at the International Exposition of 1853 in New York City as illustrated in Gleeson's *Pictorial Drawing Room Companion*, 1853. The three contraptions attached to the ceiling of the stand are baby-jumpers, which may indicate that some of the dolls' clothes represent the attire of small children. The several sewing cases do not appear to be doll-size but were probably for use by the little seamstress. The wicker cases were probably for the dolls' spare clothes and necessities. My Bloomer doll (see page 77) has her china washing set and her spare bonnets and slippers. Three American firms received an Honourable Mention for their doll exhibits, which were chiefly of dressed wax dolls. Of Tuttle's firm it was said: "The specimens of dressed dolls here exhibited certainly surpass anything we have ever seen, both in tasteful design and beauty of decoration." (Dorothy Coleman Collection)

coincided with great advances in photography and in printing practices. By the mid-19th century the popular press and magazines such as the *Illustrated London News* could carry pictures of the royal family. Victoria was interested in the arts and quite an artist herself so that both photography and etching occupied the royal couple as hobbies. A tiny etching done by the Queen herself shows little Princess Vicky at three months in her nurse's arms.

How early were the first Royal Model Baby dolls produced? We have to believe it was about 1841. Vicky herself as a child no doubt owned dolls, one of which survives (see page 53), although it turns out to be German-made. This is not surprising, since the children had so many German relatives and as a result probably received the majority of their toys as gifts from that country.

When a doll has a family history, it is often difficult to prove the attribution. It is a dilemma when a doll is stated to be a model of the Princess Royal or Princess Alice or Princess Louise (boys seem to have been less popular as Royal Model Babies), but it scarcely matters for they are sisters and bear a family resemblance. All are blue-eyed of course and have scanty fair hair, skilfully inserted in the poured wax scalp. They do convey rather realistically the plump, pale baby which seems to have been the Victorian ideal, over-clothed in layers of long gowns and beribboned bonnets. With clothes beautifully made, trimmed with lace and embroidery, they presented a whole new concept of doll play. "Little mothers" could have cradles and furniture, china tea-sets and perambulators and a "royal family" all their own (see page 101).

If, as I have suggested, the Pierotti family introduced Royal Baby dolls, they were soon imitated by other manufacturers, and the period of the finest luxury poured wax dolls had arrived. It was left to Madame Montanari to capitalize on the situation when Prince Albert had the idea of a great London trade exhibition. The beautiful Crystal Palace specially erected in 1851 and planned by Joseph Paxton was a model of contemporary engineering. John Ruskin called it "a glorified cucumber frame," but the Queen, ecstatic at the success of her beloved husband and his plans, wrote in her private diary: "The great event has taken place – a complete and beautiful triumph – a glorious and touching sight, one which I shall ever be proud of for my beloved Albert and my country." Her eldest children were present with her at the opening ceremony and must they not have exclaimed with pleasure when they saw Madame Montanari's prize-winning exhibit portraying the royal family (see page 87).

Not only did the Crystal Palace exhibition give an enormous impetus to British trade, it also sowed the seed for similar exhibitions abroad. In 1853 fine wax dolls were on show at the New York Crystal Palace Exhibition (see page 90). Did the Montanari family provide some of them? Clearly shown in the picture are Montanari-style dolls and also some of their toilet baskets made of cane.

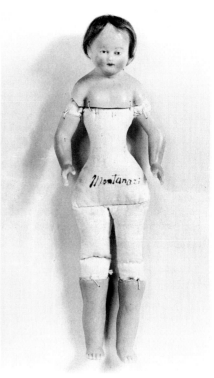

Above Montanari baby doll shown undressed, and, **left,** wearing a long baby dress with a blue ribbon, perhaps to indicate a royal prince. 1850. 14 inches. (Mrs Marianne Bodmer, Zurich)

Below Pierotti baby doll in cradle, 1880.
21 inches. (Private collection)

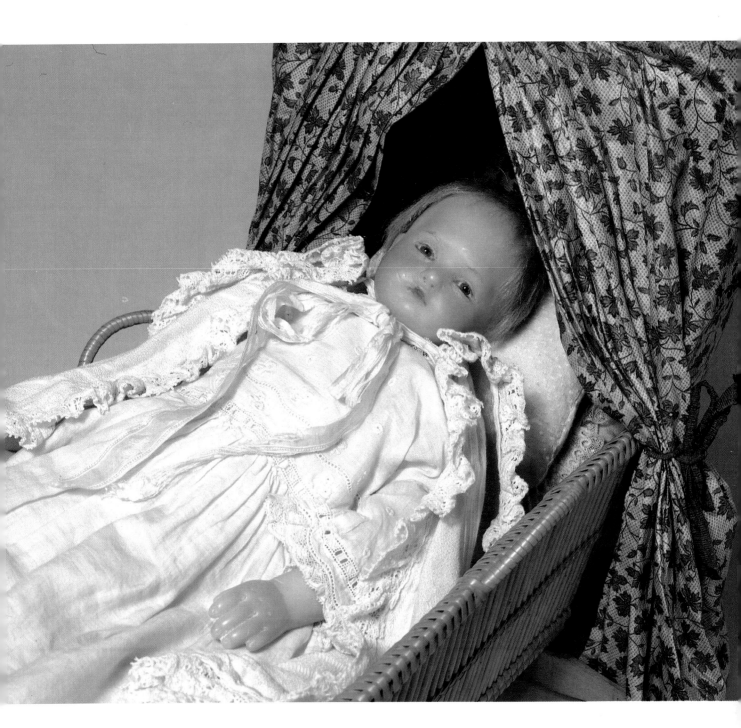

Directory of Major Wax Doll-Makers and Doll-Making Areas

In museums up and down Great Britain, and abroad, there are fine dolls without any mark or clue as to their origin, and much of the story of London wax doll-makers is full of question marks. Equally, early business directories list doll-makers about whom absolutely nothing is known, and to whom we cannot ascribe any specific models. This chapter looks at some of the best known doll-making families and concerns, tracing their history and their methods of manufacture often over several generations, and indicates as well some of the gaps in our knowledge.

Anthony Bazzoni

Although Anthony Bazzoni was in business over a long period (he is listed in London business directories between 1832 and 1855), we have little evidence of the dolls he made. He was, however, known as the inventor of the Speaking Doll. We do at least have one of the few authentic face-to-face interviews with an actual maker. In *London Labour and the London Poor* Henry Mayhew included "the ingenious inventor of the speaking doll." As it is so relevant to our subject it is worth quoting in full:

> I am the only person who ever made the speaking doll. I make her say "papa" and "mamma". I haven't one in the house now to show you. I

Opposite Christmas tree fairy doll made by the Pierotti family. 1900. 18 inches. (Bethnal Green Museum of Childhood)

Right Advertisement for Bazzoni dolls. (Guildhall Library, London)

Far right Doll marked Bazzoni with wax-over head on stuffed body, kid arms and glass eyes. This rare doll has wig and baby clothes. C.1850. 29 inches. (Shelburne Museum, Vermont)

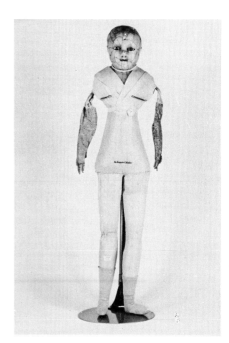

Opposite Montanari doll said to represent Princess Alice, designed from a portrait showing her driving with the Queen. C.1850. 18 inches. (Mrs Marianne Bodmer, Zurich)

Below Fine-quality wax doll, "Rosamund," in front of Sudbury Hall. Presumed Montanari, but possibly Meech; unmarked. 1863. 25 inches. (Cadbury Collection, Sudbury Hall, Derby)

have sold the last. I sold one to be sent to St. Petersburg – it was damaged on the passage and when landed couldn't say either "papa" or "mamma" and the gentleman who bought it couldn't get it mended in all Russia. I could have told him that before. For the exhibition of 1851 I believe there will be something equivalent to what I tell you of, but there will be something of everything. The invention of the speaking doll took me many experiments and much study. The thought struck me one day on hearing a penny trumpet – why not make a doll speak? Science is equal to everything. Some time ago a ventriloquist came over from Dublin to me; he could imitate everything but a baby and he came to consult me about a baby's voice. I put him in my show room and said "You stand in the corner and hear it." I made the doll speak and he said "That is the thing." He gave me two guineas for the price of the machine (not a doll) and went away quite glad. I have taken the apparatus to a party and made him speak on the stairs; a young gentleman I did it to tease turned quite white as he could not tell who or what was coming. After I determined to try and manufacture a speaking doll, I persevered day by day, thinking of it when doing other things, and completed it in three months. I often dreamed of it, but never got a hint of the speaking doll in my sleep, though I have in other discoveries. When I heard my doll first call me "papa" – which she very properly might – I said in a sort of enthusiasm – it was feelings of the greatest gratification – "I've got her at last." I sell rather more than a dozen a year at £6.6 [six pounds, six shillings] each.

Many a time in my showroom have the children looked out for the baby when they heard my doll. I had a rascal of a parrot once who could say "papa" and "mamma" as well as my doll herself – the parrot learned it from the doll. Many doll-makers have dissected my speaking doll to get at my secret. I knew one clever man who tried twelve months to copy it, and then put his work in the fire. I laugh – I don't care a fig. I have the fame and the secret, and will keep them; the profit is but small – and as for the fame, why that's not for me to talk about.

The single example of a doll marked with the Bazzoni name (page 71) is not a talking doll but has a wax-over *papier-mâché* head with a hair wig and glass eyes, and is dressed in baby clothes.

The Pierotti Family

The Pierottis can be taken as a typical example of a doll-making concern. Their work is identifiable and fine examples of their models can be seen, as well as some of the moulds and tools they used. Generous bequests to the Bethnal Green Museum and to the Toy Museum at Rottingdean, Sussex, by members of the Pierotti family, and their personal reminiscences, have given us a full picture.

The Pierottis' success was because they were a family business handing craft skills from father to son. Indeed, all the family members served an apprenticeship in modelling or assembling. The girls made fabric bodies and clothes for the dolls and undertook the onerous task of stuffing soft bodies and limbs. As the family tree shows (page 79), it was a large family.

The Pierottis originated in northern Italy in the area of Bergamo and Volterra. They seem to have been of high standing with a family coat of

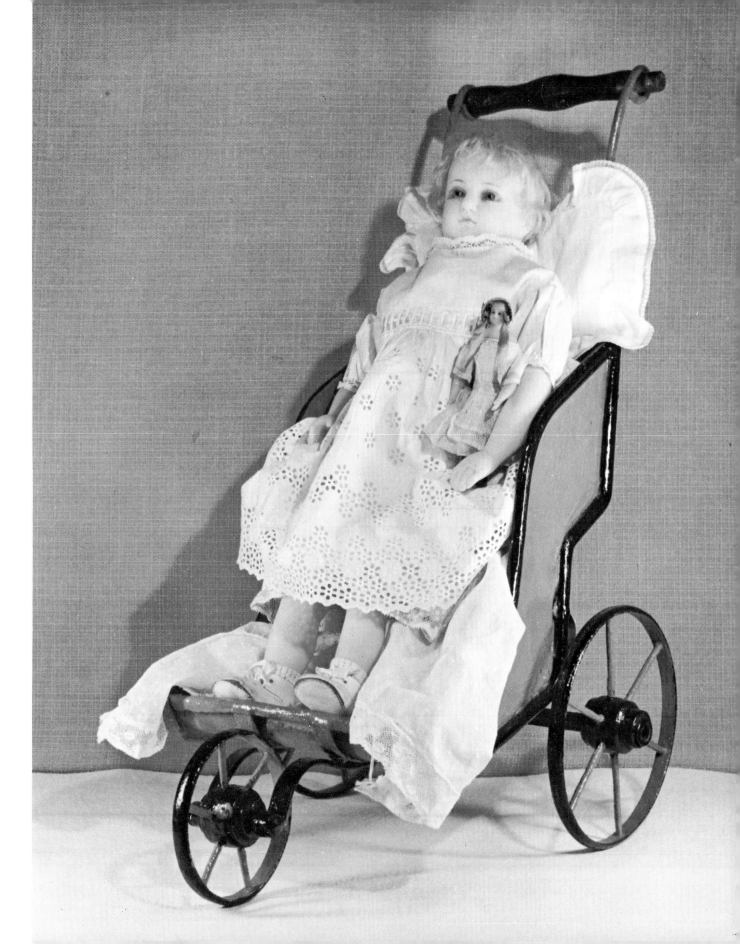

Opposite Wax-over composition Mrs Bloomer doll in her reformed costume. 1851. 21 inches. (Mary Hillier)

Right Mrs Bloomer doll dressed as the scold Mary Caudle and with a Crystal Palace souvenir pin. Wax-over *papier-mâché*. 1851. 21 inches. (Mary Hillier)

arms. Giovanni Stefano Pierotti, born in 1730, possessed vineyards at Volterra and a wine export business which probably brought him to England, as he is recorded as having married an English wife at Reading in 1750. A child of this marriage, Domenico, born in Italy, was sent to England in 1770 to receive medical attention at St Bartholomew's Hospital, London, after injuring himself falling from a tree. His mother's sister, a Mrs Castelli, who lived at Portsmouth, not only looked after the boy but also trained him in the arts of modelling and moulding. She is reported to have made milliners' figures and dolls made of *papier-mâché* coated in wax, as well as the plaster castings for wall and ceiling moulding popular at that time for house decor.

In 1790 Domenico married an English girl, Susanna Sleight, and established himself in London. He is recorded selling dolls at the Pantheon Bazaar as early as 1793, a trade he seems to have excelled at, and was naturalized in 1810. Of his very large family (five boys and six girls), the ninth, Anericho Cephas (Henry), followed his father's trade, specializing in modelling wax likenesses of prominent people and making high-quality wax dolls. It was with Henry that the family name became famous. By 1847, he and his elder brother Giovanni Dominic appear in London directories, as doll-makers and makers of plaster figures. Henry won a medal at the 1849 London exhibition, and claimed to be the inventor of the Royal Model Baby dolls that depicted the numerous children of Queen Victoria (see also page 66).

Henry set up a stall at the London Crystal Palace Bazaar at 108 Oxford Street, the present site of the Peter Robinson store. This sometimes results in family history declaring that a doll was bought at the "Crystal Palace," but the Bazaar was of course started after the 1851 Great Exhibition had ended. Henry advertised toys as well as dolls. The Pierotti family tradition that Henry modelled some of his wax dolls after his own children is borne out by their very Italianate features and, in some cases, the beautiful orange-gold Titian-coloured human hair used for coiffure. Initially, the poured wax doll had to be sculpted by an artist, and when two or three part-plaster moulds had been set from this original any number of wax models could be made. The actual apparatus was simple, and doll-making could be easily carried on as a home industry. There is evidence that others pirated Pierotti's ideas, but of course the real artistry lay in the skilful techniques used to transform a wax shell into a beautiful doll head. Warm molten wax was poured into the cast, and the surplus was poured back into the can when a thin layer had cooled and set. Colour was introduced by the addition of carmine and of white lead, which gave body strength. For a *de luxe* doll Pierotti often used a double or triple layer of wax, both to strengthen the material and gradate the colour. Once the wax head was removed from the cast the mould marks were removed and smoothed with small tools. Eye holes were cut, and the blown glass eyes placed in position from within with a small stick and fixed with liquid wax. Larger dolls were often given eyebrows and eyelashes to enhance their realism, and hair was skilfully and naturalistically inserted into the scalp by small tufts cut into slits with a scalpel. At the actual hair line, hairs were sometimes inserted singly by needle to give full realism.

Henry Pierotti died in 1871, but the doll-making business was continued by his son, Charles William, and his daughter, Celia, probably assisted by

PIEROTTI FAMILY TREE

Giovanni Stefano Pierotti *b.* 1730
m. English wife 1750 (sister of Mrs Castelli)

Domenico Pierotti *b.* 1760 (Volterra, Italy) (naturalized 1810)
m. Susanna Sleight 1790 (England)

| Sera 1792 | Susanna 1794 | Lucia 1796 | Stefano 1798 | Nurata 1799 | Anna 1802 | Giovanni Dominic 1804 | Nitilla 1807 | **Anericho Cephas** *b.* 1809 *d.* 1871 *m.* Jane Gumbrell 1828 | Guiseppi 1811 | Carlo Stefano 1814 |

| Jane 1829 | Anerico Cephas 1830 | Celia 1831 | Alfred 1834 | John 1836 | Nanna 1838 | George Henry 1840 | **Charles William** *b.* 1841 *d.* 1892 *m.* Anne Roache 1859 *d.* 1932 | Helena 1848 | Jessica Maria 1851 | Cephas 1852 | Walter 1853 |

| **Charles Ernest** *b.* 1860 *d.* 1942 | Arthur 1862 | Alice 1863 | Alfred 1865 | Florence 1867 | Rose 1869 | Joseph 1870 | **Harry** 1872 | Albert 1873 | Augustus 1875 | Maud 1879 | Beatrice 1882 |

From records furnished by Miss Irene Pierotti

Opposite A standing proof that Madame Augusta Montanari modelled actual Queen Victoria dolls. This fine portrait doll is signed on the lower torso with her name and Soho Bazaar. There is real braided fair hair, dressed with seed pearls and artificial flowers. Fabric body, legs and feet. 1851. 24 inches. (Museum of London)

Above This treasure is a valuable Montanari doll called "Selina" and was bought in the Paris Exhibition of 1855. The forehead is rather bald, with the hair inserted towards the base of the crown. She is gazing downward, with blue eyes set in with sculpted lids. The dress is of beautiful ice-blue satin. The decoratively fringed hat has ornamental pale blue chenille pipe-cleaning wire. Montanari won a medal at the Paris Exhibition, and this is a splendid example, with Montanari fashion down to the tiny seed pearls. It is sometimes said that the initial M is marked inside Montanari heads. I have never found it – but then I have never had many heads off! 1855. 23 inches. (Tunbridge Wells Museum)

Above Pierotti model of King Edward VII as a Field Marshal. 1901. 21 inches. (Wenham Museum, Massachusetts)

other members of the large family. Dolls were made for Queen Victoria, and on one occasion some tiny wax figures adorned a cake made for one of the royal weddings. Charles also undertook display work and made models for hairdressers' and tailors' models. He married in 1859 and died young in 1892 of lead poisoning – one of the dangers of working with wax but probably unrecognized at that time. Helped by two of her sons and three of her daughters his widow carried on the business at home in their house at Shepherds Bush, West London. The finished dolls were transported the few miles to central London in a hansom cab, to be sold at various West End shops such as Hamley's, Morrell's and F. Aldis (see page 66).

I am indebted to a direct descendant of the family, Miss Irene Pierotti, for her personal reminiscences. She recalls regular visits as a small child to her grandmother's house at weekends, when she watched, fascinated, her "uncles" Charles and Harry at work: "dear kindly old men," busy in the big kitchen where a huge cauldron was warming on the kitchen range, with the unforgettable scent of wax wafting through the house. There were boxes and boxes of eyes, plaster moulds lined along the shelves and some arranged on the long bench ready for the next batch of heads and limbs. The impressions of childhood are vivid, and so she remembers too the family Christmas and the little wax angel she was given off the top of the tree. A laden pear tree dominated the back garden in summer, and there were wonderful cakes on the tea-table spread for a large family of visiting grandchildren. Her aunts and grandmother, who worked until she was 90, were busy cutting out the calico for the doll bodies, machining the pieces together and stuffing the finished sections. The dolls were always dressed by hand, and their pretty faces were hand finished and dusted with starch powder or violet powder to give complexion (the fine "bloom" of a new wax doll). A little touch of rouge was rubbed on their cheeks and their ears with wadding, and finally lips, nostrils and ears were dry painted with a small brush.

Under Charles Ernest, the firm continued to make baby dolls in the Pierotti tradition, but produced original models as well. Miss Pierotti possesses a brown wax doll Charles made for a fortune-teller at a bazaar, and after the Boer War he reproduced a portrait figure doll of "Bobs," Lord Roberts, Commander-in-Chief in South Africa and hero of Kandahar in the earlier war in Afghanistan (see page 65). The uniform was meticulously copied and imitation medals and decorations added. Just how clever an artist Charles was is demonstrated by the large model made of King Edward VII at his coronation. The monarch is shown to the life with moustache, beard and balding crown carefully depicted (see page 64). One suspects this was given exhibition prominence, but its history is lost.

After the First World War, wax dolls lapsed in popularity and were replaced first by china and then by plastic types. Charles carried on working until he retired in the 1930s when he was over 70, maintaining an agency for repairing old wax dolls. His tools and some examples of his work and materials may be seen at the Rottingdean Toy Museum, Sussex, and fine dolls that confirm the enduring skill of the Pierotti family are exhibited in museums world-wide.

The Versatile Montanaris

Possibly the best known name among wax doll-makers is that of Montanari. Among early collectors it seems to have been almost the *only* name, and any poured wax English doll was called either a Montanari or a Montanari-type. This was especially so as a result of the publicity given to Augusta Montanari's winning exhibit at the Great Exhibition in 1851, and because dolls have occasionally been found with her signature scrawled across their fabric body.

Until recently, the origins and background of the Montanari family have been shrouded in mystery, although it had always been my feeling, based more on her style of needlework and fashion and her obvious enthusiasm for royalty than on any proven facts, that Augusta Montanari was probably English. It was especially gratifying to me to discover proof in the 1861 census returns. Augusta Montanari was born Charlotte Augusta Dalton in Grantham in 1818. Her husband Napoleon, born in Corsica as one might suspect from his Christian name, was six years older. Besides the elder son, called Richard Napoleon like his father, who became a wax modeller himself, there were three other children, Julie, Constance and Charles Albert Victor Augustus. One wonders sadly what became of the children when their mother died of consumption in 1864, and whether they themselves survived childhood. Richard is recorded as having been born in New York, which proves that his mother and father must have been living in the USA.

The first record of Napoleon Montanari as a wax-modeller dates from 1849. One of the Pierotti family recalls that her father as a small boy in the 1860s remembered Montanari coming to visit his father; indeed the two families lived not far apart. Montanari was apparently a tall, very good-looking man and was thought to be South American; the child imagined he was an actor. Miss Maude Montanari, the last surviving granddaughter, has also confirmed that she thought her grandfather came

Below Modern copy of the death certificate of Madame Augusta Montanari, who died of phthisis (consumption). (Mary Hillier)

CERTIFIED COPY OF AN ENTRY OF DEATH						Given at the GENERAL REGISTER OFFICE, SOMERSET HOUSE, LONDON.		

The statutory fee for this certificate is 3s. 9d.
Where a search is necessary to find the entry, a search fee is payable in addition.

Application Number 01359 4

REGISTRATION DISTRICT Kensington

1864. DEATH in the Sub-district of Kensington Town in the county of Middlesex

No.	When and where died	Name and surname	Sex	Age	Occupation	Cause of death	Signature, description, and residence of informant	When registered	Signature of registrar
479.	Ninth May 1864 10 Lancaster Road	Augusta Montanari	Female	46 years	Wife of Napoleon Montanari modeller	Phthisis 1 year Certified	Richard Montanari Present at the Death 10 Lancaster Road Kensington	Tenth May 1864	G. R. Dames Registrar

CERTIFIED to be a true copy of an entry in the certified copy of a Register of Deaths in the District above mentioned.
Given at the GENERAL REGISTER OFFICE, SOMERSET HOUSE, LONDON, under the Seal of the said Office, the 29th day of November 19 67.

DA 523579

This certificate is issued in pursuance of the Births and Deaths Registration Act, 1953.
Section 34 provides that any certified copy of an entry purporting to be sealed or stamped with the seal of the General Register Office shall be received as evidence of the birth or death to which it relates without any further or other proof of the entry, and no certified copy purporting to be given in the said Office shall be of any force or effect unless it is sealed or stamped as aforesaid.
CAUTION.—Any person who (1) falsifies any of the particulars on this certificate, or (2) uses a falsified certificate as true, knowing it to be false, is liable to prosecution.

Left Portrait of the doll-maker Herbert John Meech. (Private collection)

Opposite Bride doll. Unsigned, but probably Meech. 1870. 19 inches. (Bethnal Green Museum of Childhood)

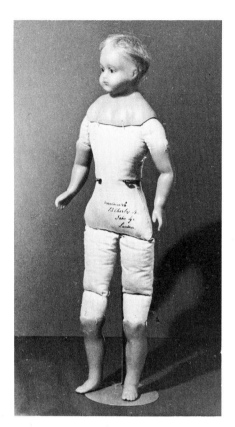

Above Unclothed baby doll marked with the Montanari name and "13 Charles St, Soho Sq, London." 20 inches. (Madeline Merrill Collection)

from South America. Certainly some of his earliest and best models would lead one to believe that he had first-hand experience of Mexican types. A visitor to the display at the Great Exhibition wrote:

> The beautiful groups of Mexican figures exhibited by Montanari in the Fine Art Court, daily attracted a throng of admiring gazes. They were indeed very interesting as illustrating town and savage life in Mexico in all their phases. Amongst them the most remarkable were a grotesque figure of an "Aquador" (water carrier), a "Remendor" or street cobbler in his ragged attire, a "Confessional" group of three figures, a group of two Indian women dancing a fandango on the green, while the leper is playing on his guitar, and the scene in the courtyard of a farm, with the wealthy farmer and his lady about to set out on a journey. A beautiful group of Mexican fruits (50 in number, natural size) formed an interesting feature.

One detects, surely, the hand of Madame Montanari in some of the costuming, for that was indeed her *forte*. A model of a North American redskin about to scalp a traveller was also shown, and another of an Indian on the point of carrying off a child. Finally, there was a gruesome full-size figure of a person "in the last stages of consumption," which makes one wonder if there was some history of this dreadful disease in the family.

Miss Montanari recalled that Napoleon Montanari also made a model of the famous Siamese twins Chang and Eng, who were a great popular success when they were exhibited in London.

> In each engraver's shop one sees
> Neat portraits of "the Siamese"
> And every wandering Tuscan carries
> Their statues cast in clay of Paris.

One could well believe that Augusta Montanari rather identified herself with the young Queen Victoria. She was practically the same age, and her first child was born in 1840, when the country was rejoicing at the arrival of the Princess Royal. Queen Victoria was horrified at the speed with which she achieved a large family, and remarked that little babies were "frog-like" and ugly until their little bald heads were "hidden with a pretty bonnet." Augusta Montanari, who could produce such pretty replicas in wax, probably felt that she owed her success to a constant production of royal babies. Indeed, she gave her last child a very royal name.

Pierotti claimed to be the originator of the Royal Model Baby, but there was so much popular interest that other wax doll-makers followed suit. There was no lack of illustrations in contemporary newspapers to show just how the babies looked. Royal progeny were the major impetus to the production of luxury wax dolls.

By 1851 and the Great Exhibition, the Montanaris must have been working hard, probably helped by their son, who actually exhibited himself at the Paris Exhibition in 1855. They must have been proud indeed to gain medals both for the Mexican models and for the doll exhibit. The *de luxe* edition of the *Illustrated London News* described the exhibits.

> In the North Transept Gallery, Class 29, Case 122, were a rich display of model wax and rag dolls by Madame Montanari. These playthings

Above Engraving of the Montanari show case at Great Exhibition, 1851. *The Illustrated London News* reported: "A large glass case before which there is always such a crowd of Mammas and little girls that a male critic seems an intruder. It is impossible to conceive a more charming fairy court. There is a quaint little nudity who stands up in front, like Puck among the fairies. . ." Some of the dolls represented children of the royal family, others children from America and Africa in appropriate dress. There are also examples of Montanari rag dolls, "largely patronised by Her Majesty for the Royal nursery." (Mary Hillier)

are indeed very beautifully modelled: the hair inserted into the head, eyelashes and eyebrows. The represent the different stages of childhood up to womanhood and were arranged in the case so as to form interesting family groups. They include portraits of several of the Royal Children. The interior of the case represents a model drawing room, the model furniture being carved and gilt and elaborately finished.

The report added that an adjoining glass case showed "the newly invented model rag dolls, peculiarly adapted for the nursery, for their softness and durability and largely patronized by those who are connoisseurs in dolls' flesh." The only adverse comment was that the dolls were intended for the children of the wealthy rather than for general sale. Undressed dolls cost from 10 to 105 shillings, and the dressed ones were very much more expensive.

Signed examples of Montanari dolls show that at one period Madame Montanari had a stall in Soho Bazaar. Other dolls were given the Charles Street address where she worked and lived (see page 86). Charles Street was a small turning out of Soho Square, close to the Bazaar and now vanished. Napoleon was always listed as a wax-modeller in the London Directory and Richard Napoleon called himself a wax artist. It was the *panache* with which Madame Montanari dressed her dolls that made them stand out. She used the finest lacey socks and little hand-made slippers, and as well as being in contemporary fashion the design of the costume had many personal touches. A water-colour design at the Victoria and

Opposite This doll, with its sophisticated dress of mulberry coloured silk, may have been made by Meech. It has defined features, sculptured eyes and lids. The auburn hair, which may have been trimmed, is made of rather strong, stiff human hair caught in a bun at the back. *c.*1870. 19 inches. (Tunbridge Wells Museum)

Right Doll marked with Meech's oval trademark, Kennington Road. Muslin with blue ribbon and lace, very forget-me-not blue eyes, pretty pannier skirt. *C.*1865. 23 inches. (Museum of London)

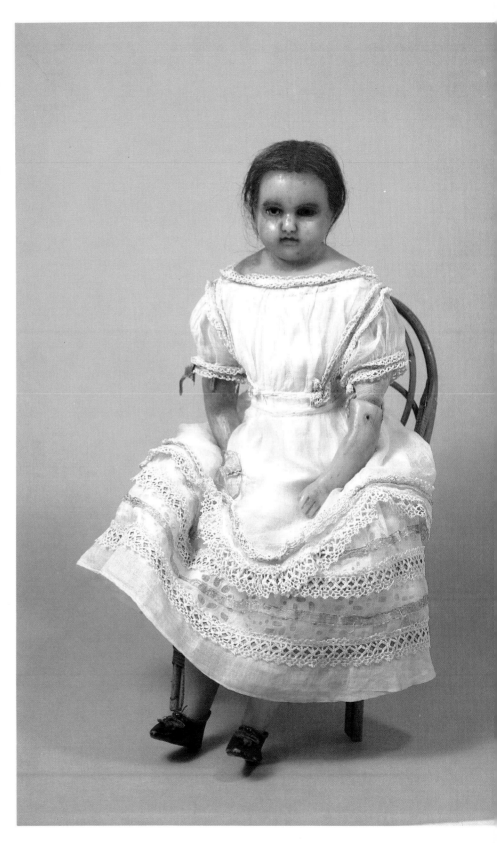

Above Montanari London rag doll. The mask face has a fine muslin covering, and the whole head is covered, with the bonnet attached. There are little, black, pin-point wax eyes and wisps of human fair hair around the edge of the bonnet. The original gown has the V-shaped yoke that perfectly imitates the baby dress shown in prints of the royal baby. The outer band of the original gold leaf medallion celebrating Augusta Montanari's award has the "A. Montanari Class XXIV. Exhibition prize model 1851. Ich Dien" (the royal motto – "I serve"), and profiles of the royal pair, Victoria and Albert. So the doll must have been sold soon after the Great Exhibition in 1851. 13 inches. (Museum of Childhood, Edinburgh)

Right Princess Louise model doll shown at the London Exhibition in 1853. 14½ inches. (Bethnal Green Museum of Childhood)

Albert Museum illustrates her artistry; the ribbon bows and rosettes are her personal signature. She loved all the exquisite millinery of mid-Victorian fashion: the fringes and lace, the braidings and beadwork. She used tiny seed pearls for necklaces, bracelets and coiffeur, and the V-shaped yoke employed on both baby gown and stylish robe was very pretty as well as a serviceable needlework doll pattern. The materials used were the best obtainable and for that reason have often lasted wonderfully well.

Did Augusta exhibit at the New York Exhibition of 1853? The Exhibition catalogue commented that "the specimens of dressed dolls certainly

Right and far right Unsigned doll with poured wax head, arms and legs, and a cloth body with a tiny waist. The clothing is original and so elegant that it suggests Madame Montanari. The outer dress, with a wide, low neckline and short flared sleeve, is of ivory sheet wool with much decoration and trimming of picked cherry red silk ribbon, matching cape sleeves, and soutache braid trim on cummerbund and upper sleeves. There is a cherry velvet wired hat, an ivory silk ribbon and the remains of a white ostrich plume. A red silk buttoned purse is attached to the waist with a red ribbon bow on the wrist. The doll has openwork socks, flat black leather hand-sewn shoes, leather soles pencilled "8" on bottom, with a flat black ribbon and metal buckle over instep. The underclothing is also exceptionally fine, with hand-sewn linen drawers, narrow at the knees with five tucks and *brodérie anglaise* trim; linen chemise; plain wool flannel tucked petticoat with two rows of feather-stitch trim; linen petticoat with twelve rows of tucks; and *brodérie anglaise* insertions. The costume may possibly be a copy of a fashion plate of the period, *c*.1850, and is similar in style to the one shown on page 116. 19 inches. (Lorna Liebemann Collection)

Above Reduced-price "favour ticket" to "Mr. Montanari's Royal Exhibition of Wax Work Models." (Westminster City Library Archives Department)

surpass everything we have ever seen both in tasteful design and beauty of decoration." If the style is not Montanari herself it must surely have been in imitation, as the Tuttle print on page 67 indicates. As has been seen, the Montanaris and their son certainly exhibited at the 1855 Paris Exhibition, where Madame claimed that the wax would resist the temperature of hot climates.

Socially, 1855 was an exciting year in London. The Emperor Napoleon III brought over his beautiful new wife on a state visit to Windsor. Eugénie was tall and elegant with auburn hair and a marvellous complexion, token of her Scottish ancestry – a great contrast with the small-statured, plump Victoria. In England she wore a crinoline of grey with black lace and pink bows and a wealth of chrysanthemums in her hair. Madame Montanari, one feels sure, did not miss the details, nor did she resist a chance to portray such a trend-setter. The state rooms at Windsor were inspected by the Queen and the imperial bedroom designed in honour of the royal visitors. The bed curtains were of violet satin (Eugénie's favourite colour) topped with feathers and finished off with golden eagles and the letters "LN" and "EI" embroidered in brilliant green. When the Paris exhibition opened that August, Queen Victoria and Prince Albert were invited to France to pay a return visit. Did they pause at the Montanari case? And was Madame Montanari there in person? One can only imagine the scene.

A very intriguing bargain ticket (left) probably issued in mid-1856 gives some clue to the affairs of the Montanari family after the excitement of the exhibitions. Some of his Indian models and her dolls were used for a waxwork show staged in the Linwood Gallery, and there is an allusion to the French visit that cemented the friendship between Victoria and Eugénie.

The Linwood Gallery, housed in an old building in Leicester Square, once the home of Sir George Savile, had formerly been famous for the exhibition of amazing needlework pictures done by a Miss Linwood in imitation of Old Masters. It opened in 1816 and ran until her death in 1845,

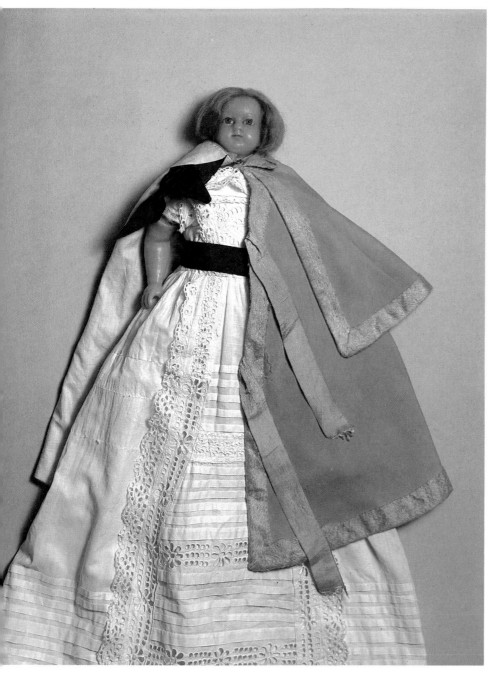

Left Doll marked "Marsh (E. Moody Soho Bazaar)." The hair is reddish blond mohair set in groups of two or three hairs at the hairline and in tufts and ½-inch slits as it approaches the back; centre parting, as Marsh usually did. The eyes are cornflower blue, the duck-egg blue carrying-cape is of plush silk with mourning ribbons. 1860/70. 17 inches. (Museum of London)

Opposite Poured wax doll stamped front and back with Marsh's stamp (Sole Manufacturer – like the Pierottis' *sole monifactura*). The doll was gowned in Paris by one of the famous doll dress-maker shops in a plain early 1870s gown of deep-blue silk taffeta trimmed with yards of delicate black lace. There is a dust ruffle, of course, and the dress is laced from the back. The blond mohair is set in tiny groupings with inset hair eyebrows, large blue glass eyes, pierced ears and finely-modelled, large poured legs and arms. The body shape is plump. C.1870. 27 inches. (Lorna Liebemann Collection)

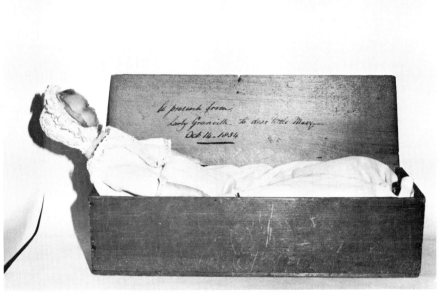

Above Label from box containing Montanari's prize winning baby doll of 1851. The baby doll was a prize "Model Muslin" doll. (Mrs Marianne Bodmer, Zurich)

Right Montanari London rag doll given in 1854 by Lady Granville as a present to a child. The box is original. 13 inches. (Cadbury Collection, Sudbury Hall, Derby)

and was considered one of the sights of London. After the pictures were sold, the place deteriorated and became, in the words of a contemporary critic, "A Noah's Ark of Entertainments." It was popular for a time for the *tableaux vivants* of Madame Warton, which she called Walhalla. Oddly, these *poses plastiques*, as they were called, were a sort of waxwork in reverse. Motionless human actors posed to represent statues and were powdered or painted completely white to represent Parian marble. It was said that such charades were first invented by Madame Genlis of Paris (a friend of Madame Tussaud) in the 18th century, and one wonders if she was in turn inspired by one of those fine waxwork shows with life-size figures where the audience might comment "all they lack is breath to make them live!" The exhibition of flesh in place of wax was of course rather more entertaining, and one suspects in the Warton show of being an early forerunner of "striptease," especially since Lady Godiva was named as one of the cast!

There seems to be no contemporary report on the Montanari exhibit at Savile House, and it is not known how long it lasted there. The old house itself was burnt down in 1864, the year that Madame Montanari died. Leicester Square was the centre of the amusement parade of London. In 1859 a wonderful American circus, Howes and Cushings United States Circus, performed there and a musical chariot (an Apollonicon) harnessed to 40 cream horses drove the length of the road to give it publicity. Waxwork shows were becoming less popular, and were being ousted by new delights. The circus included a company of true North American Indians who danced their war dance and exhibited their whoops and horsemanship.

Richard Napoleon Montanari married in 1875 and had a large family although only two children survived to adulthood. Both he and his father exhibited in Paris in 1878, and Richard Napoleon remained famous for his London rag dolls. From the reference in her advertisement, he must also

Above Cartoon guying Mrs Bloomer from the *American Reformer*. (Mary Hillier)

have assisted Mrs Lucy Peck (see page 140). Napoleon seems to have vanished; perhaps he went abroad again, or even stayed in Paris. His grand-daughter, born in 1886, did not remember him, although she recalled the wax dolls being made at her home at 3 Rathbone Place, London, just across the road from Soho Square where Richard's mother marketed her first fine dolls. A modern office block has replaced this house, but similar ones still stand alongside the Old Black Horse pub next door.

It must be concluded that Madame Montanari relied on other dolls for her exhibitions as well as the expensive poured wax models. For some of the character dolls she dressed she may have used the wax over *papier-mâché* London doll familiar in the first half of the 19th century. The illustration on page 77 shows such a doll dressed as Amelia Bloomer, the American reformer. Her clothing is exquisite, both the tailored costume that Mrs Bloomer suggested should be adopted by women who wished to be the equal of men, and the period bonnet and frock. The brimmed hat and the frock are both in the Montanari style. Mrs Bloomer came complete with her own fine Staffordshire toilet set and a souvenir pincushion with an embossed design of the Crystal Palace. She was bought by the Duke of Northumberland at the Great Exhibition for his children, and eventually passed down as a Montanari to the children of his gardener who, as they grew up, cherished it and looked after it because it was "from the Duke." *They* were never allowed to play with it, but the Duke's family created a new role for it and called it Mary Caudle, after a character in a well-known book of the period. Its clothes are embroidered with a tiny "MC."

Although wax-over dolls of this type are very similar, they none the less achieve odd variations of character. Some of them look pleasant and humble, others rather haughty or a little mean. Others again have a stupid expression or even look downright scatty. It all depends on the final hand-touching of the features. To the children who played with them, the dolls did assume very real personalities – as fundamental as those later favourites, the Teddy Bears. I just detect in my doll a certain smugness as if she were saying "…but I knew Madame Montanari." How I wish she could also speak!

MONTANARI FAMILY TREE

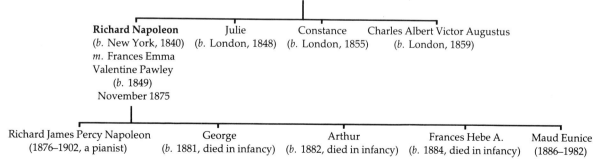

Opposite Tall, German-made wax-over doll (perhaps made in Sonneberg) with very elaborate coiffeur of real hair with a net over it. This is a German style seen in some of the lustre dolls of 1860/70. The dress is of commercial net, but is prettily decorated with coral bows, and beneath the stiff full skirt pretty mauve boots are painted on plump composition legs. The arms and hands are wooden. 22 inches. (Tunbridge Wells Museum)

Right Doll dressed *à la Watteau* as depicted in an advertisement by Cremer published as supplement to *Englishwoman's Domestic Magazine*. 1865. (Miss Faith Eaton)

DOLL A LA WATTEAU
From an original figure, Expressly designed by
JULES DAVID *and dressed by* CREMER JUNIOR
210, Regent Street for the
Englishwoman's Domestic Magazine

Above This unmarked doll has a replacement wax head set on a French doll body after the original china head had been broken. 21 inches. (Sotheby's)

Opposite Meech doll in fine costume with the Meech label "Dollmaker to the Royal Family." It has fixed blue eyes, long, fair brown hair and thick eyebrows and eyelashes. 1890. 23 inches. (Worthing Museum and Art Gallery)

The Meech Family

"Doll maker Herbert John Meech was an individualist. Not only did his dolls have certain unique characteristics but he, himself, lived apart from the colony of doll makers." So wrote Jo Gerken in 1964 in her *Wonderful Dolls of Wax*. "We are left with the feeling, that, artist as he was, he would be uncomfortable with his present relative anonymity." It is true that dolls made by Meech invariably bear his stamp and sometimes add the proud information that he was appointed doll-maker to the royal family – a Royal Warrant-Holder, in fact. We also know that his workshop was situated in south London, just below the river in Kennington Road and not so far from the Edwards factory in the Waterloo Road. Both areas were in easy reach of the West End and the luxury shops and bazaars that sold wax dolls.

I have been fortunate to find, still living in that same area, present-day descendants who can fill the gaps in Meech history and explain the relationships in a family involved in wax doll-making over a considerable period.

Herbert John Meech was the son of John Meech, a sawyer, of Buckland Newton in Dorset. He was born in 1833 or 1834, and at a quite early age he was sent to London to live with an aunt in Bayswater. Why it is not known, but perhaps he was a bright child, and it was thought he would have better opportunities in London. Certainly the boy seemed to have initiative. It is said that even as a child he entertained his friends with a toy theatre performance for which he charged a farthing admission! He started work early, and at 15 had a job in a hardware store. He seems to have been ambitious and presently found a job in Madame Tussaud's Waxworks at Baker Street. He was about 17 when the famous old lady died, and presumably he continued to work under her sons. But by 1852, at the age of 19, he had set up his own small factory in Kennington and was employing several people.

In 1851, when the Great Exhibition in London was such a success, there must have been additional publicity about fine wax doll-making, and perhaps Meech saw the opportunity to branch out in a lucrative business with his new-found skills in wax-modelling. At the Tussauds rooms he must have learnt very thoroughly the techniques and the materials necessary. It is not known whether Meech continued to do any modelling for the Tussauds after he had transferred to his own factory, especially since Madame Tussaud's talented grandchildren carried on the modelling themselves. One might feel certain, though, that he attended the gala opening of the new Tussauds in 1884 at the special gallery on Marylebone Road, for the young man had profited from mixing with the gentry who visited the Exhibition and were now customers for his luxury dolls.

In 1858 H.J. Meech was living, perhaps as a lodger, at Tower Street, Southwark. On Christmas day of that year he married Eloise Cox, the daughter of Samuel Cox, an auctioneer, at the nearby church of St George the Martyr, close to his Kennington Road premises.

Of this marriage there were four sons and two daughters. The eldest son, Herbert, never worked for his father, but the other three did, especially Ernest John and his wife Lily, who carried on the business into the 1920s after its founder had died. As is often the case with a self-made man, H.J. Meech had a reputation for being stingy and a hard master. He seems not to have got on well with his sons, and perhaps he in his turn

Left Commercially dressed wax doll *à la Watteau*, made by Edwards and resembling Cremer's advertisement. *C.*1860. 24 inches. (Mrs Jean Ogilvie)

Opposite Pottery doll toilet set and furniture. 1850/70. (Mary Hillier)

THE OPERATING TABLE.

Above *A Day in a Doll's Hospital:* illustration of the operating table in Marsh's workshop from *Strand Magazine,* 1895. (Mary Hillier)

Right Early 20th-century photograph of the Manchester Doll Hospital. The shop dates from 1833 and later became a doll's hospital. (Manchester Public Libraries)

Above *A Doll Vendor,* painting by Henry Nelson O'Neill ARA, sold at the artist's studio sale at Christie's, June 18, 1880, and at Mrs Hudson's Christie's sale on December 12, 1938. The pretty girl seems to be proffering the finely-dressed wax doll with a list of names. Perhaps the scene is a charity bazaar and she is hosting a competition such as "Guess the Doll's Name." The curtained booth seems to be in a garden with details of a tent background. Other dolls and toys are shown at the rear. (Christie's)

resented the fact that his family never had to work as hard as he had. Edgar seems to have set up a business on his own, he and his family having quarrelled with their father and moved away.

H.J. Meech himself lived to a ripe old age and died aged 82 in 1916. A grand-daughter, Florence Éloise, came to live at 4 St Faith's Road, West Dulwich, to care for the old man when her grandmother died. Next door, at number 2, lived Herbert Arthur Meech, the eldest son, who never took part in doll-making, but was able to dip into a bag of memories for his descendants since he lived to his 92nd year. He also retained an interesting example of his father's work. H.J. Meech was asked to model two wax Madonna heads for a Roman Catholic church, and kept one mould for himself, which was exhibited on a stand beneath a glass shade. This beautifully fashioned head, which may have been sculpted from his wife or daughter, was unfortunately stolen.

In 1890 the London Directory listed Meech Bros at 112 Fore Street, E.C., City of London, and gave the information that they made tailors' dummies and milliners' models. It is not known whether this company was two of the brothers working apart from their father, or merely an offshoot of his business. But from information I have been given by P.J. Meech, it is clear that early in the 20th century Edgar Henry John Meech was carrying on a business making wax dolls and display figure heads at an address in Aliwal Road, Clapham Junction, and also, unexpectedly, at Eden Quay, Dublin. Maybe Irish collectors will come up with examples of Edgar Meech dolls! P.J. Meech remembers helping to make them during the 1920s.

> I remember the heads and small arms, and bodies were moulded on wooden blocks with *papier-mâché*. This was pasted over the blocks and then wax was kneaded over the dry models. Hair was added, eyelashes, brows etc. One of the small jobs I was given was to put a small hook shaped object in the coal stove for Father to use to mould

Above Wax dolls probably made by Edwards, illustrated in Silber & Fleming's trade catalogue. 1883/4. (Christie's)

the eye sockets in the head. I remember also that Grandfather gave me a large tin of porcelain eyes to pick out a pair of a same colour to match the colouring of the model being made. Colouring was obtained by the use of different chalks ground in a marble bowl with pummel [pestle and mortar]. Head, limbs and arms were held together with a fine twine threaded into holes previously made in the *mâché* and wax. My grandmother made clothes for the figures.

P.J. Meech also remarked that, as he and his sister were twins, his grandfather made life-size figures in their likeness to stand in the porch and "confuse visitors."

H.J. Meech's early dolls are of very fine poured wax, and some of those I have seen are beautifully dressed. They are also strongly tooled and have rather heavy features, as for example the sombre expression on page 00. The dolls made by P.J. Meech's grandfather were not poured wax but wax over *papier-mâché*. It seems that Meech's business had declined by the end of the 19th century, when imported fine European dolls were presenting too much cheap competition to luxury wax dolls.

MEECH FAMILY TREE

John Meech (sawyer Buckland Newton, Dorset)

Herbert John Meech (wax modeller 1833/4-1916)
m. Eloise Cox 1858

| Herbert H. *m.* Mary Parker | Ernest John (1860-1927) *m.* Lily | Edgar Henry John | Arthur | 2 girls |

Herbert Arthur (1889-1982)

Edgar Henry John

P. J. Meech 1918-

| Florence Eloise (1885-1939) | Alfred (1886-1952) *m.* Catherine | Harold (1895-1952) *m.* Florence Allen | Doris 1898- | Albert |

Lily   Dennis *m.* Joan 1926-

Audrey *m.* Denis Mahoney 1927-

| Michael 1954- | Colin | Amanda | Anne 1953- | Rosamund 1956- | Hilary 1958- | Jeremy 1962- |

Julie 1977-   Natalie 1979-   Sebastian 1982-

Above Groups of dolls from Baghdad of assorted types and sizes; 16, 18, 21 and 26 inches. In 1868 Mrs S. G. Herbert, wife of the British Resident-General C. L. Herbert, was very distressed to find that the ladies in the Harem did little but feast on sweets and quarrel. She had the idea of importing some dolls from London and interesting these ladies in dressing them in the current fashions. It is amusing to imagine the scene, and the result is very picturesque, as the ladies used miniature ornaments and coins, metal thread and very pretty materials. Mrs Herbert asked for four dolls, all different, and was sent three German-made, including an engaging Mottschmann type, and one English (on the right), who succeeds in looking rather haughty and slightly superior. Mrs Herbert may have requested cheap dolls since none of them is the pretty but more expensive poured wax type available at that date. All the dolls shown here could have been bought at Cremer's. (Tunbridge Wells Museum)

Right Cremer twin dolls professionally dressed in blue with ric-rac braid. Marked on body "Cremer Junior MAKER." 1870. 16 inches. (Mrs Marianne Bodmer, Zurich)

Below Two little German wax-over dolls probably dressed in Paris and bought by Lady Potterton there in 1871. 1871. 12 inches. (Mary Hillier)

The Marsh Family

As a young child in the 1920s, I remember being taken to a Dolls' Hospital somewhere in Fulham, where we lived. Sadly, I can recall little about it other than the strong smell of simmering glue and a vague picture of miscellaneous doll parts scattered on the bench. Was it the little shop carried on by Jessica Marsh? It could well have been. The Dolls' Hospital at 114 Fulham Road has long since been swept away, and the small shop replaced by a rather affluent decor shop. But descriptions remain of the time when it was the busy centre for repairing doll "accidents." In 1883, the magazine *Little Folks* suggested that almost any repair could be effected, and mentions the "modeller" who could "take a piece of clay in his fingers

Above W. H. Cremer's advertisement in Peter Parley's *Annual*, 1866. The shop at New Bond Street was under royal patronage. (Mary Hillier)

and with a few simple tools work it into the desired form, using an uninjured limb as a pattern. Over this clay model he will pour some plaster of Paster and thus obtain a mould." The article details the various injuries wax dolls received, and adds that new hair could be inserted on a bare scalp, or in the most serious cases on a new head. "New Heads are kept in stock just as legs and arms are and it is frequently found easier and cheaper to provide a doll with a new head than to repair a damaged one."

One presumes that the doll doctor was Mr Marsh, but twelve years later another article in the *Strand Magazine* gives a good and rather humorous account of Dr M. Marsh MD (Mender of Dolls) whose husband was a wax-modeller. A drawing shows a young woman at work who could have been young Jessica Marsh. "The Doctor chats away kindly and communicatively to her children customers." She was very merciful and "never applied the needle more than was necessary, never wasted a drop of spirit used for washing their faces." Of course this account does not answer the questions we would really like to ask. But it does relate that on the walls hung a number of portraits of the doctor's intimate friends (wax dolls), "and one of them is of a splendid large doll which was sent to America." This must have been 24 inches in height since its size may be compared with a little prize pug dog photographed on a couch alongside.

Marsh dolls were certainly sent to the USA, and one of them is shown on page 93. It is not known whether Charles Marsh was William Marsh's brother or son or, even whether they were related at all, although their names appear together in the London Directory of 1864. After the death of Charles Marsh it seems that his widow and daughter carried on a repair business only. The fine clothing on the earlier Marsh dolls was probably made by the family. The dolls themselves are fine large models and especially "English" looking in their features and colouring. Most have blue eyes and flaxen hair.

W.H. Cremer & Son

W.H. Cremer's first London shop was in fashionable Bond Street, and was advertised by its owner as a German Toy Warehouse. One can speculate that the family had German origins, and it is clear from their trade and their travels that they had strong associations with the doll-making area of Sonneberg and acted as agent for toys and dolls in London.

In 1862 Cremer showed toys at the London Exhibition, and it must have been soon after this that a fine and prestigious toy shop opened at 210 Regent Street. A pretty coloured plate issued with the *Englishwoman's Domestic Magazine* in 1865 showed a fine wax doll dressed "à la Watteau," and gave instructions about making such clothes. It is not clear whether this was a German or an English doll, but the very beautiful poured wax doll (see page 97) in similar fashion and bought in about 1860 seems to indicate it was from London. Cremer was an agent for some of the famous wax-making firms: Pierotti certainly and quite probably Edwards as well. The charming twin boy and girl dolls shown on page 105 bear the Cremer mark and state that he is a wax doll-maker. But it seems more likely that he had a workroom making up supplied wax dolls and costuming them prettily.

In 1875 W.H. Cremer Junior, in a small illustrated booklet probably issued as an advertisement, refers to the English "waxen beauties." He

Opposite German wax-over composition baby doll with *Holzmasse* mark made by Dressel. 1880. 24 inches. (Mary Hillier)

Below German wax-over composition doll from Sonneberg with voice box accompanied by a French Schmitt doll. Late 19th century. 20 inches (Sonneberg doll) and 18 inches (Schmitt doll). (Mrs Heather Bond)

compares a cheap wooden doll with the dressed dolls seen in the 1871 London Exhibition, at which Edwards exhibited (see page 117).

The Little Red Riding Hood, the young lady dressed for her first party, the flower girl. Their beauty was almost ravishing. That of Red Riding Hood would I am sure, have laid quiescent the most ferocious of gobbling-up wolves. And the clothes of these fair ones! What choice materials and how admirably fitted. Didn't the young ladies at the first party envy that profusion of lace and the pretty dimple faced flower girl with green satin underskirt and light silk tunic? Did she have one flower left after ten minutes solicitation? The other young lady belonging to this charmed circle was nestled away, I suppose sleeping, in the half opened drawer of her cabinet. We could just see her trousseau, comprising, apparently, everything necessary and every luxury of toilet to which she could possibly aspire – morning dresses, walking costumes, riding habits, carriage robes, evening dresses, ball dresses, velvet and sealskin jackets, silk, satin and leather boots to lace high above the ankles, with brocaded slippers and parasols fringed, laced and tasselled – all of the most expensive description and an abundant store of other components of a lady's trousseau: the underclothing all hand made. Her dazzling jewellery and such dinner and tea services of silver gilt and finest Worcestershire were as only the highest in the land could place before their guests.

Below Exhibition doll: recumbent child. 19 inches. (Cadbury Collection, Sudbury Hall, Derby)

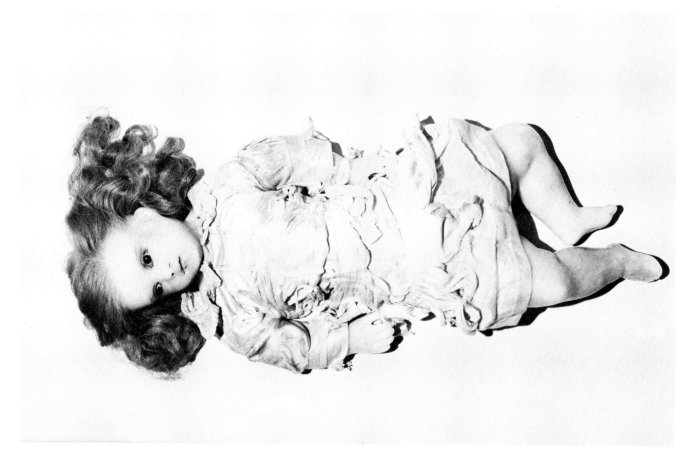

Above Page from *The Toys of the Little Folks* by W. H. Cremer, Junior, 210 Regent St, London, 1875. (Mary Hillier)

After this positively Dickensian wealth of detail, Cremer continues with a comment that can only refer to the Montanari London rag babies (see page 87):

> It was here we also saw some of the handsome baby dolls in wax and rag for which we are so deservedly famous. But you couldn't detect the composition in the latter class. There was a softness in the face, a porousness about the skin that was not perceptible on the wax dolls. Plainly dressed in long clothes and hoods all so well made that they could be taken off for the laundress as often as might be necessary – how thoroughly babyish they were. Mammas might have claimed them for their own and irascible bachelors fainted at their feet!

W.H. Cremer Junior seems to have been an exceptionally ambitious and ingenious businessman. He was also the all-round entertainer who promised that he could organize every sort of party whether games and the distribution of presents, Punch and Judy shows, fireworks in the garden or adult *fêtes* complete with marquee. He could arrange magic lantern shows, dances, acrobatic displays and sessions of magic or ventriloquism. One speciality was a cornucopia employed for issuing "gifts from Paris, Berlin, Vienna" at children's parties and one visualizes him kept constantly busy at the luxurious social life of late Victorian London.

In another account, he claims that he was instrumental in collecting European toys for the 1871 Exhibition. Indeed he was officially thanked for his role in organizing the exhibits after the problems presented by the Franco-German war. Cremer mentions a visit he paid to Sonneberg, when he met Adolf Fleischmann (1819-95), one of the doyens of the German doll-making trade and a member of the much inter-related Dressel-Fleischmann-Müller family, which flourished throughout the 19th century. At this time in the 1870s, Fleischmann was partner with one Carl Craemer, to whom the London Cremers may have been related, having at some time anglicized their surname.

The Sonneberg Doll Industry

The doll-making industry in Sonneberg, Thuringia (now part of the German Democratic Republic), remained important until the Second World War. According to the Ciesliks' article in *Doll Reader* (Fall 1984), the American firm of F.W. Woolworth bought the business of Wilhelm Dressel in 1913, and in 1925 they built a handsome warehouse for doll exports to the USA, which was eventually blown up in 1945. One financial reason for the endurance of doll-making during the inflation years of the early 1920s in Germany was the stability of American dollars, enabling firms trading with America to continue in business, and American doll-makers to design dolls to be made up cheaply in Germany.

Some 100 years after W.H. Cremer's visit to Sonneberg, Mrs Jo Gerken was there contacting some of the remaining descendants of the most famous doll families for her book *Wonderful Dolls of Papier Mâché*. Her account is invaluable, since it demonstrates how closely inter-related the families were. Born with doll-making in their blood, they inherited traditionally well-organized factories. The famous firm of Dressel seems to have been founded in about 1730 by Johann Paul Dressel (1709-38). In 1732 he married Sophie Fleischmann, and the son of their marriage was Johann

Opposite Two-faced Bartenstein wax doll
with sound box worked by strings at the side
and metal hood for bonnet. Patented in 1881.
23 inches. (Bethnal Green Museum
of Childhood)

Below Page advertising German *Taufling*,
published *c.*1850. (Private collection)

185

Above Two scenes from doll-making in the Sonneberg district, 1896: *Stuffing Bodies* and *Waxing the Heads*. (Mary Hillier)

Opposite German doll-making methods as illustrated in *The Wonderland of Work* by C. L. Matéaux, 1880. (Mary Hillier)

Philipp Dressel (1735-1804). This man's son, Ernst Friedrich (born 1797), had eight children, including the famous brothers Cuno and Otto Dressel (born 1829 and 1831) and sisters who married into other doll families. An involved family tree of cousins and numerous brothers and sisters ensued, of which Mrs Gerken gives a full and fascinating account.

Round about Sonneberg whole areas were devoted to doll-making. On Cremer's visit, he named Friedenbach, Neustadt and Schalkau as having 3000 or 4000 inhabitants each, who scarcely did anything else. The workers included those who did the rough work of tree-felling, turning, pulp-making, and so forth, as well as those involved in modelling and sewing. In 1870, Cremer stated that 2 million dozen dolls were made and exported annually from Thuringia. Adolf Fleischmann told him that not less than 32,000 people were involved, including the women who made little chip boxes and did the colouring. Mrs Molesworth, the famous Victorian writer of children's stories, spent part of her childhood in Germany. She herself apparently did not care a lot for dolls, but she did use her knowledge of German doll-making villages in some of her stories. In *The Toymaker of Bergstein*, she sketches a village family where the mother is fixing doll wigs and the father is engaged at the doll factory. A visiting English child is so enchanted with a head with lovely hair that the cottager promises she will acquire the body for it complete. In another story set in London, Mrs Molesworth reports on a doll delivered from "Marshalls" (Marshall & Snelgrove, a famous Victorian store). "Wax dolls," she writes, "in those days were the only pretty ones. But there are two or three kinds of wax. There are some that open and shut their eyes and others a good deal larger, but which don't cost any more because they don't open or shut their eyes."

In *The Wonderland of Work* (1880), a children's book on industry illustrated with fine wood engravings, C.L. Matéaux wrote about the "large school of design" in which dolls were studied and techniques improved, and also refers to the division of labour, each worker specializing in one part of the production process. He also comments on the fact that the men seem to smoke their large swing pipes non-stop and on the pretty blue-eyed girls with fair plaits invariably dressed in the local fashion and neatly bonneted. In this particular workshop the doll heads were dipped in wax when they had dried – "the more dips the better the lady's position as a wax doll is likely to be" – and were dusted with the sweet-scented bloom of violet powder which "makes them look like fresh-gathered peaches." This factory was clearly producing good-quality dolls, since the hair was pressed into the wax scalp by the roots and some of the dolls were also given eyelashes. It could well have been in the Dressel works that some of the prettiest German wax dolls were produced.

A report in a German magazine of 1896 of a visit to the "Doll Town" of Sonneberg gives a lively picture of the scene in a small workroom of a "family" business. In one of the illustrations a burly workman completes the production process of pouring liquid wax from a jug over each head. The hair wigs of angora goat wool were stuck on to produce a cheaper type of doll altogether – perhaps like the rosy-cheeked play doll illustrated on page 122.

The making of *papier-mâché* material was a closely guarded secret, and presumably used a variety of substances. In 1917, an English trade

Opposite Praying doll made by Edwards and shown at the 1871 Exhibition. The modelling of hands, fingers and nails is beautifully detailed. The body is of soft fabric with metal eyelets where the limbs attach. There is real hair inset, with curled, real eyelashes and brows. The eyes are carefully set with a contemplative look. 17 inches to the knee. (Mary Hillier)

Above Plate from the supplement to *The Queen*, October 24, 1874, the "Lady's Newspaper and Court Circular." The fashions of the day dictated from Paris were gaily shown in ladies' papers such as *The Queen* and *Harper's Bazaar*. French artists found coloured lithography especially suitable for their fine plates, and the accompanying text gave details of style and material: cheviot velvet; blue velvet skirt (for the effeminate little boy with his row of model soldiers and cannon), grey poplin, claret cashmere; plain velveteen skirt; fur trimmed velveteen polonaise. No details are given of the fashion of the dolls shown, but

there is a new baby in lacy wraps and a seated jointed doll with fair hair in black with a ruby coloured sash. Like the children and their mother, all wear hats, flower-trimmed, like that of the French doll Violet (see page 126). It is clear that playing with dolls was a popular pastime, and just as with today's girls who play with Sindy and Barbie the wardrobe was most important of all. Dolls took part in the fashionable promenade of Parisian life. They were the spoiled inhabitants of the curtained saloon, early introduced to the etiquettes of an artificial society. (Mary Hillier)

Right Wax-over composition German "pumpkin-head" dolls with wooden arms and legs. 1860. 10 and 17 inches. (Sotheby's)

Opposite The "Westwood" baby doll. This wax nativity figure with painted eyes and mouth was given by Thomas Westwood to his wife Eliza on January 2, 1844. He feared that his wife was unable to bear him children – in fact she had 17. The doll was passed to Eliza's daughter Ethel on October 7, 1884, and then to her grandchild Rosemary in 1938. Frail German wax dolls, prettily dressed and presented in tiny chip boxes, were used for many other reasons besides religious ones, and were presumably a cheap and popular "bazaar" doll line. 1844. 6½ inches. (Worthing Museum and Art Gallery)

magazine *Toy and Fancy Goods Trainer* published some recipes under the title *German Doll Making Secrets Disclosed*, obviously with the aim of spurring English makers to take over a trade that had been predominantly German. All the preparations used a pulp of soaked or cooked paper waste. The paper first passed through a "devil" or shredding machine. To the prepared pulp was added whiting (ground chalk), Plaster of Paris and liquid glue. The maker might increase the bulk variously, according to the waste products obtainable, by using rye flour, cotton waste (cellulose), linters (mattress flock or old rag), and so forth. One maker in Vienna used waste from a Meeerschaum pipe factory and another trimmings from a kid glove factory. The usual proportions recognized were pulp, two parts; whiting, three parts; Plaster of Paris two parts; and glue water to mix. To produce a material that would set unbreakably hard and not crumble, a small addition of sulphate or alum or potash was added (about 2 per cent of

Below Portrait of John Edwards' infant daughter, Maud. Half doll on wooden base, with bonnet and dress added for reality. 1883/5. 12 inches. (Museum of London)

Opposite Model of Princess Louise, daughter of the Prince of Wales (later Edward VII) and Queen Victoria's grand-daughter, in her wedding dress. Louise was born in 1867 and married the Duke of Fife in 1888. 24 inches. (Mrs Graham Greene, Rotunda, Oxford)

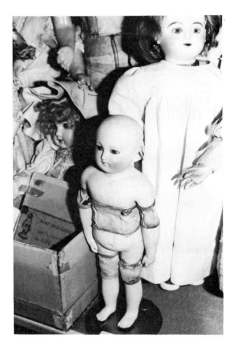

Above A doll with porcelain parts, sold at auction, showing the so-called Mottschmann construction. (Sotheby's)

the total). Sometimes a deterrent against insects or rats such as nicotine dust or "colocynth" juice from the bitter gourd was added.

When the Sonneberg Museum exhibited some of its treasures in London in 1980, including the famous scene of *Gulliver in Lilliput* constructed by Fleischmann for the Great Exhibition, the catalogue named some of the most famous "modellers:" Peter Hetzel, Heinrich and Gustav Stier, Rudolf Wagner and F.M. Schilling. It was Heinrich Stier who also invented lead pendulum eyes, to give weighted sleeping movement, and ball and socket joints for composition dolls. According to Jürgen and Marianne Cieslik in their book *Puppen Sammeln* ("Collecting Dolls"), Heinrich Stier visited the USA in about 1852 and then studied doll-making in London with a leading wax doll-maker, gaining useful information about wax-working. He went on to introduce these methods in his own factory in Sonneberg making wax-coated doll parts. Stier's sister Barbara married one of the Schilling family, and after she was widowed Stier set up business with her in Coburg. In the last quarter of the 19th century some of these same names appear in patent listings.

It would be interesting to know if the Sonneberg records trace any connection between the Schmidt firm of Sonneberg and Schmitt et fils (Maurice and Charles) of Paris. The last named, who had a workshop outside Paris at Nogent-sur-Marne, near Vincennes, and a shop in the centre, took out a patent in 1883

> to guarantee the new idea of applying directly to bisque a layer of animal, vegetable or mineral wax used alone or mixed with other substances such as paraffin or stearin. Wax to be applied to heads and busts of dolls and baby dolls waxed after they leave the oven. This will make a very lifelike appearance as well as make the dolls more durable.

They had already won a silver medal in 1878 at the Paris Exposition for their Bébé Schmitt. This curiously constructed little doll, 18 inches high (see page 109), has a ball-jointed body marked with the Schmitt crossed hammer mark and also the name Du Magasin des Enfants, Passage de l'Opéra, Paris. The waxed head is fastened from the top of the crown (hidden by the wig) over a socket neck. We know that earlier in the last century French makers used German parts and it is possible that Schmitt, like Fleischmann, had a connection with the factories in Sonneberg. One suspects that the family network of Geman doll-makers was very widespread, with representatives in the USA, Britain and France.

Mottschmann Dolls

At this point I would like to add a word about so-called "Mottschmann" dolls. The term is now applied to a whole class of dolls issued in numbers and great variety, especially at about the middle of the 19th century. One example found in the Braunschweig Museum, in Germany, bore the patent mark:

Patent 29 April
A. D. 1857
Ch. Mottschmann
Sonneberg.

Opposite Cheap German wax-over composition doll in its original packing. 1850. (City Museum and Art Gallery, Worcester)

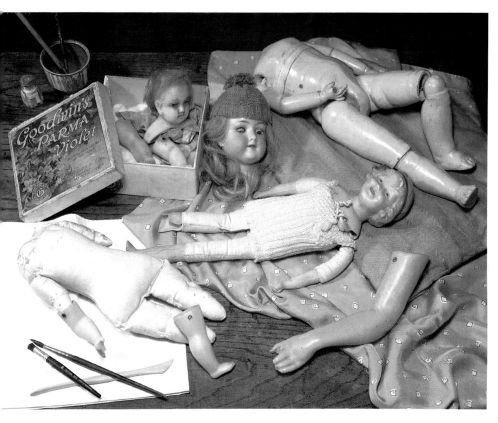

Above Relics from Mrs Lucy Peck's Dolls'
Hospital, including a dismembered Pierotti
doll brought for repair and a single "Lucy
Peck" arm. 1920. (Mrs Norman-Smith)

Opposite "Evangeline" doll designed by
Elinor Glyn for the heroine of her novel
Vicissitudes of Evangeline. 1903. 24 inches.
(Mrs Heather Bond)

THE TRIMPEY COLLECTION

"I love old dolls – the playthings of a gentler age: with rosy cheeks and sparkling eyes, they wonder where the Children are, who held them close in years gone by." So wrote Mrs Alice Kent Trimpey, one of the early collectors who amassed antique dolls purely for the pleasure they gave and for nostalgia for the past. Proud of her pioneer ancestry, she was born on a farm on Sauk Prairie in Indian territory. But from childhood on she lived for most of her life at Oak St Baraboo, which she pictures in the books she produced: *Story of My Dolls* (1935) and *Becky: My First Love* (1946). The books are now collectors' pieces and so are the photographs of the dolls that illustrate them. The dolls and photographs are now in the collection of the State Historical Society of Wisconsin at Madison.

Mrs Trimpey liked to indulge her eccentricity of dress and unconventional behaviour, but she wrote well and the photography by her beloved husband E. B. Trimpey was up to professional standard. Her stories of the past warmed the American heart and certainly fostered a new generation of collectors. Some of the old dolls Mrs Trimpey owned were certainly of European

origin, and their history is always interesting. Mrs Trimpey was described as as "old fashioned as dried apple sauce" by a contemporary. At the time she wrote, there was of course little scientific research into the makers of dolls and she would have cared little anyway.

"Violet", **below**, has an interesting history. She is a large doll, 27 inches tall, and has been well looked after by her original owner and re-dressed in a similar *mode de Paris* in pale blue merino trimmed with white lace and ribbons, with original leather boots. The doll was said to have been bought in Paris at a shop owned by Monsieur and Madame Couchard (untraced) by an American for his three-year-old niece. The tiny blue locket set with pearls also belongs to this baby. The most interesting clue is that the doll was said to have been made at a small factory in Rue du Temple, which might reasonably have been the important firm of Pannier, 140 Rue du Temple. Maison Pannier was one of the few French firms that advertised wax dolls between 1870 and 1892. Madame Blanche Pannier was renowned for her millinery and wigs, and she helped to organize the French exhibit at the Vienna Exhibition in 1873, where she won a medal.

The firm used a little parasol as trademark, Charles Pannier having invented little parasols for dolls. Rue du Temple was in the very centre of the French doll-making area, and the firms there emphasized beautiful clothing.

Opposite Major Dupont and Persis. According to Mrs Trimpey, Persis was a "Montanari type," while Major Dupont resembles Prince Albert, although he is wearing an American uniform.

Since this was publicized, every doll with loose limbs and a soft abdominal section with a voice box has been classified as Mottschmann. It is unfortunate that in doll-collecting half-understood information is often eventually adopted and established as fact. A researcher tentatively puts forward a discovery and a theory, and in no time others have eagerly added it to the certainty of doll history. Such a case is Mottschmann, for I am sure that the patent was applied specifically to the *apparatus* that worked the eyes and the voice box, by twin strings emerging at the hip, and was used as an improvement to an already existing type of doll.

The first curious baby doll in this style was called a *Taufling* in Germany. (This is literally an old-fashioned word for an infant at baptism, like the English *chrysom*. I suppose we might say new-born.) Such dolls were sold in simple little gown shifts, as clearly and prettily shown on page 00. There can be little doubt that this original version of the doll was copied from similarly constructed Japanese dolls. Whether this was at the time of the 1855 Exhibition, when Japanese dolls were exhibited, or whether it was rather earlier is very difficult to prove. Various interesting legends are attached to these charming little dolls. In her book *Schönes Spielzeug* ("Beautiful Toys"), Dr Pieske suggested that they were invented by a Herr Finger and called *Finger'sche Puppen*. Jürgen and Marianne Cieslik put forward a claim for Herr Edmund Lindner who, it seems, visited the Great Exhibition in 1851. He bought a little Japanese doll either there or when he stopped in Cologne on his way home, and when he returned developed small German dolls based on the Japanese pattern. Like the Japanese doll it

Right Modern wax doll of Christopher Robin with Pooh and Piglet made and dressed by Margaret Glover. 1980. 19 inches. (Mrs Margaret Glover)

had a squeaker inside and wore a short shirt. Because the dolls had no shoes or socks they were sometimes called *Barfussler* (little bare-footed one). Later, many other makers imitated this popular doll and issued improved varieties. This seems a likely version, since the Lindner family had existed in Sonneberg as doll-makers since 1835 and were related by marriage to the Dressel/Fleischmann family, eventually amalgamating their concern with Fleischmann.

In the museum at Leiden, where the collection brought back from Japan to Holland by Dr von Siebold is lodged, there are Japanese dolls of this sort dating from about 1820. They are almost always represented as little boys, since the Japanese esteemed baby boys so greatly. They have male genitalia and the typical style of little boy hair, with a tuft each side above the ear and a central tuft trained at the centre crown. Whoever copied the

Above illustration to "An Evening Hymn" from *The Playmate* magazine, April 1864:
  Good night my father, mother dear
  Now kiss your little son;
  Good night my friends, both far and near;
  Good night to every one.
(Mary Hillier)

doll left out the genitalia in the German pattern but retained an oriental look by using painted wisps of hair. The hard pelvic section and the hollow arm and leg sections with so-called 'ski-pants' design, the swivel head cupped on the neck and shoulder unit, and the moulded hands and feet all imitated the Japanese dolls. Japanese originals usually have the large big toe separated from the other toes where the strap of the *geta* (the Japanese wooden sandal) fitted.

What is really interesting is the way the doll was improved and elaborated in Germany. Examples are found with carved wooden heads, made of moulded *papier-mâché*, or fine ceramic and with a very pretty variety of moulded bonnet and hat patterns coloured under wax. Some versions were given maturer faces than the "baby" or *Taufling* type, with wigs and fancy costume. The picture on page 109 shows a doll very similar in proportion and style to a Mottschmann but lacking the string movement. She has blue, weighted, sleeping eyes, six painted bamboo teeth in an open mouth, a pressure voice box and measures 24 inches.

It is curious that the original Mottschmann used the English word *"Patent"*, rather than the German *geschützt*. Perhaps he was intending to export his dolls to Britain or the USA or to show them at a European exhibition, and feared piracy. Or maybe he himself had "borrowed" the idea of a "speaking doll" from some earlier inventor such as Bazzoni. Cheap German dolls continued to be made with a "squeaker" in their stomachs, but more luxurious dolls later had more sophisticated "voices."

John Edwards
Curiously, although the names of Montanari and Pierotti are familiar to all those interested in wax dolls and examples with the mark of such makers as Meech and Marsh turn up occasionally, Edwards dolls are almost unrecognized. They are anonymous because they were not marked at the factory where they were made. Presumably the trade was mainly a

Right Portrait of the three daughters of John Edwards. *C.*1885. (Julian Edwards)

wholesale one, supplying the famous London toy shops of the period. Yet we know from contemporary reports that John Edwards must have produced more wax dolls than any other manufacturer. His output was very varied, from beautifully dressed dolls of the very highest quality to, at the other end of the scale, quickly made little dolls sold cheaply.

It is not known whether John Edwards was related to the Charles and Henrietta Edwards who ran a doll-making concern from various addresses in Goodge Street from 1853 onwards. If he was, this might explain how he first learned his trade. John was the son of Thomas Edwards and was born

No. 64½   FORM OF LABEL TO BE ATTACHED TO OBJECTS SENT TO THE INTERNATIONAL EXHIBITION OF 1871.

DIVISION II.—MANUFACTURES. CLASSES 8, 9, & 10.

This Form should be filled up and if possible attached to the object to which it relates. It is desirable that each object should also bear a number corresponding with the number of this label to provide for cases in which the label might possibly become detached, or in which it might be inconvenient to fasten the label to the object itself.

DIVISION II.—Class No. *10* to which the object belongs. {Consecutive number of Object} No. *100*

1. Name of object   *Girl at Prayers*

2. Exhibitor's Name   *John Edwards*

3. Address   *39 & 45 Waterloo Road*

DOLL MANUFACTORY,

39 41 43 & 45 Waterloo Road
London, March 20 1877

Top Entry form completed by John Edwards for the 1871 International Exhibition. (Mary Hillier)

Above Letterhead of John Edwards' "Doll Manufactory", just south of the river Thames in Kennington. (Julian Edwards)

in Bristol on 3 November 1831. He attended the Queen Elizabeth Hospital School from 1841 to 1845, a Bluecoat School, and later in life he made a wax doll costumed in the school uniform that was given to the Bristol Museum. Surviving members of his family remember him living in a fine house at Esher, Surrey, situated in some 4 acres of land. From his portrait, done when he was about 60, he looks a fine and successful man, and is recorded as a god-fearing church-goer, as the praying child would suggest. The photograph on page 129 was taken in about 1885 and shows his three small daughters, Gertrude (born 1878), Violet (1879) and Maud (1882). The model of the child's half bust (see page 120) was designed at about the same time. The family recalls proudly that Edwards' dolls were delivered to the royal family, and the messenger (not John Edwards himself) was allowed to take them up to the nursery and hand them over to the royal children in person. (These would have been the children of the Prince of Wales, later Edward VII, and thus Victoria's grandchildren.)

According to a report in the *Graphic* in December 1871, Edwards made 20,000 wax dolls per week. "We are not a great toy making nation but we admittedly beat the whole world in dolls." Edwards had recently been noticed for the fine dolls he exhibited at the London Exhibition in 1871 (see page 117). His model was of the very finest quality with translucent wax and curled baby human hair set singly, like the eyebrows and eyelashes. It is made up like a doll, with the poured wax head, arms and legs sewn to a stuffed fabric body and is very much in the reverent and sentimental mood of the period.

Edwards' factory seems to have been established in about 1868, when he advertised that he was the "Inventor of the Exhibition wax model dolls, wax and composition dolls, wholesale and for exportation, dressed or undressed. Also the Exhibition rag doll."

An anonymous contributor to the *Little Folks Annual* in 1883 described the factory as occupying a six-floor building, with the street floor devoted to the sale of the dolls. Local children crowded round to admire the display in the factory windows facing on the street. The variety was considerable:

131

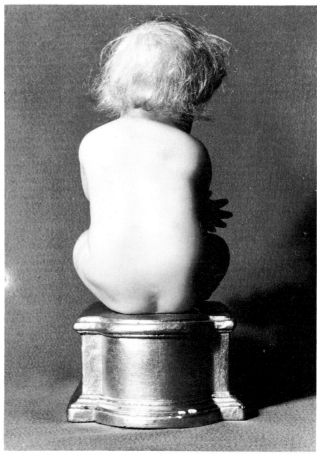

Inside the shop, counters and stands are crowded with dolls, some fully dressed and others whose outfit is left to be determined by the purchasers. There are young lady dolls of large size, attired in morning, dinner or ball costumes; there are baby dolls, most elaborately dressed in sewed muslin and lace; and there are character dolls, such as Mother Hubbard, Red Riding Hood, Highlanders and fishwives. In a special compartment are to be seen models in wax of single figures and groups copied from well-known paintings or engravings; and mechanical dolls which move their heads and imitate breathing by means of clockwork. In a show room on the next floor there is more work of this kind to be seen, and mingled with it are many curious illustrations of the wax modellers's art – casts of faces taken from life, and some also taken after death; models of persons whom fame or notoriety has brought into prominence; fancy models for displaying the wares of the milliner or illustrating the styles of the hairdresser and so forth.

Since the article is not illustrated it is interesting to read the whole description. At the time of this visit, the factory was dealing with a large order for India. This consisted of an extensive array of dolls dressed "according to the quaint styles of those artists who have distinguished themselves by illustrating children and their ways." One thinks

Above John Edwards' distinctive "E" trademark.
(Julian Edwards)

immediately of Kate Greenaway and Walter Crane. Presumably the dolls were intended for the children of India's rulers, for at that time many British families lived there.

A few years earlier, in 1876, George Bartley of the Victoria and Albert Museum, who was compiling a report on the British toy industry, visited the factory. He gives a useful and scientific account of what went on upstairs. The wax used was pure East Indian as that was cheapest and the most satisfactory for doll-making. It was melted in large vats which stood in containers of water heated to boiling point by jets of gas. It was not uncommon for a hundredweight of wax to be melted at one operation. As it was the special aim of the English doll-makers to give their dolls' faces a truly child-like expression, the original clay model was very carefully worked, and then three-part plaster moulds were made of the original. A workman dipped a can into the vat of melted wax and used it to fill some dozen moulds. The wax that remained fluid was carefully poured back, leaving the hollow wax head in the mould. Arms and legs were made in the same way, which hardly differs from the home-made process of, say, the Pierotti family.

In Edwards' establishment, skilled workmen and women specialized in their own particular part of the doll-making process. The crude rough wax head was produced with just the eye sockets indicated, and it was left to a specialist to cut eye sockets, adjust the glass eyes within the hollow head and set them with wax. In some dolls, "sleeping eyes" were adjusted with weighted wire. Wax was then run over the front of the eye and the eyelids and eyebrows were modelled by hand. The fleshy hue was already in the melted wax, but the surface of the face had to be smoothed and trimmed of any mould marks. Finally came a "severe brushing over the surface with violet powder the effect of which is really remarkable," to produce a matt surface resembling the downy bloom of a child's cheek.

The hair work was done by women, and for many of the best dolls "the hair and its insertion cost as much as the rest of the head put together." It was a fairly lengthy operation. The head to be adorned was placed on a block. Then the woman held a bundle of hair cut to a prescribed length in her left hand and with a little tool (called a "stipple" and like a flattened bodkin) she proceeded to press the roots about 1/16th of an inch into the wax. She did this manoeuvre some eight or ten times and then took a little iron roller and gently but firmly rubbed it across the surface closing the small gashes. The hair was methodically inserted in this way a few strands at a time, in rows from the nape of the neck upwards until the head was covered. Finally, the locks were curled with a tiny pair of curling tongs.

Although a certain amount of human black hair was imported, fair hair was more popular. This was flaxen-coloured mohair and was manufactured by one London house that not only supplied Edwards' factory but also the best French and German makers. It was probably Speights of Finsbury Court and Dewsbury, Yorkshire, who made the hair. They were famous wig-makers, besides advertising dolls' hair. Another outside specialist manufacturer was Messrs Gibbs of Clerkenwell, just north of the City of London, who supplied leather dolls' shoes. A baby Edwards doll has been found with a leather shoe marked with his initial E. Some fine English glass eyes were used, but for most of the cheaper dolls eyes were imported from Germany.

Bartley's informative article also describes other, cheaper dolls made in the Edwards' factory. Some were of composition dipped in wax, while others were called London rag dolls, made by a method invented by the Montanari family (see pages 83-95).

The composition was made from sheets of coarse paper soaked in starch water to make them solidify and harden when dried. The heads or masks usually seem to have been manufactured outside the factory by piece-workers, and there was a store of hundreds on the premises to be used as wanted. The out-workers had a mould of hard metal over which they forced the west pasteboard, forcing the material into every crevice with a sort of pestle. Using one mould for the face and one for the back of the head, they joined the two halves when dry to produce a tough head that could be painted and dipped into wax and transformed into a beautiful doll. For these cheap market dolls a different method was used for adding the hair: the technique, known as "slit-head", persisted from much earlier times. The workwomen sat by a small gas stove and heated several pairs of curling tongs. One woman skilfully curled ringlets and handed them to another, who in the meantime had cut a deep central gash in the doll's head into which she inserted the straight ends of the hair, sticking them in place with a blunt knife.

Few examples of "rag dolls" remain, and those that have survived are not impressive since they were designed for very young children and took the worst of nursery wear and tear. Wax was used to make a little face mask in a prepared mould. The hardened wax mask was placed on a piece of thin muslin, laid over a second mould and gently pressed down with a round rammer. The muslin adhered like a skin and gave the wax a soft and pleasing appearance less liable to damage. Features could be painted on, and cheeks tinted with rouge, and a pretty bonnet hid the joint to a stuffed fabric head and body. The dolls were usually given a cheap gown matching the lacy bonnet, wrapped in silver paper and sold for sixpence at cheap bazaars.

George Bartley also reported on the economics of manufacturing. For the finest dolls it seems that women were employed in the factory, but for cheaper ranges out-workers in the East End of London supplied stitched-up calico bodies from yards of material given out by the factory. Arms were also sewn by out-workers, whose poor rates of pay were as follows: for large arms, 6 inches long, sixpence halfpenny a dozen pairs; for small arms for cheap dolls, a penny halfpenny per dozen pairs. The arms were made from linen above the elbow and from leather below with indicated fingers. It was a pitiful trade, often undertaken by poor unfortunate women handicapped by a large family of children who, as soon as they were capable, assisted her in the handwork. It is interesting, none the less, to find such details in a report written as late as 1876, as usually dolls with this kind of body are considered to have been made much earlier in the century.

The Wheelhouse Family
The one piece of information we have about the Wheelhouse family and their doll-making activities comes from a curious interview given to a reporter from the *Toy and Fancy Goods Trader* in May 1910. Mr Wheelhouse of the Waterloo Road was reported to be one of the last of the English wax doll-makers. He considered that the industry had been ruined by foreigners. "Before the advent of German china dolls there were over 100 hands employed here – my father, grandfather and great-grandfather were all practical doll-makers." Mr Wheelhouse added that his great-grandfather had invented movable eyes, not, that is, the primitive wire pull that projected about the middle of the doll's ribs but the weighted variety that produced a sleeping eye. He also added that "every little tuft of hair on our dolls is put on separately. The wax is heated to melt it, and the hair taken from a rabbit or other skin and put in bit by bit before the wax hardens again." This method does not seem to be in line with the one used by artistic wax doll-makers of the Victorian period, but perhaps the reporter somehow got confused.

In the same issue of this trade paper, there is a short description of doll-making, in which it is explained that the method had not changed for years. Lead or plaster moulds were still used, and the liquid wax was poured into them. This seems to suggest, however, that some form of composition was also sometimes used, poured into the moulds from a faucet. When the final transparent white wax coating had dried, the heads were given a coat of bright pink paint by dipping and resembled "a boiled lobster." In an oddly period touch the reporter added that, "Some of us found that out for ourselves when we surreptitiously sampled the cheeks of our sister's idol in lieu of forbidden sweets, *not dreaming that the streaks would show!*" The bodies of these dolls were stuffed with cork shavings if they were expensive models, or with hair, excelsior, cotton waste or sawdust if they were cheap. The great majority were sold undressed as many mothers liked to dress their child's doll themselves or even to teach their daughters to make the clothes.

Lucy Peck and her Dolls' Home

The researcher relies so much on other people's memories that it is a special bonus when a surviving member of a family comes forward with photographs and anecdotes. I was fortunate to find Beatrice, the grand-daughter of Mrs Lucy Peck. Beatrice was proud of this famous wax doll-modeller – one of the last Victorian artists – and rounded off her story with information from some of the artist's notebooks in her possession. She remembered her grandmother well (who died aged 84) and her home decorated with large classical portrait busts modelled by the old lady in her last years.

Lucy Peck was born in Islington, north London, on March 22, 1846, where her father, Benjamin Brightman, was a butcher. He had married her mother, Abigail McNamara, in 1845 when he was 21. By 1847 the family had moved to 18 Duke Street, Adelphi, where another child was born on January 8, 1847: Lucy's sister Elizabeth, known as "Lizzie." Not a lot is known about the childhood of the two little sisters, so close in age, but it is believed that they attended boarding school at some stage and became governesses later. We do not know where Lucy acquired her modelling skills, but as she grew up in the West End of London one might suspect that she had tuition from a family skilled in wax doll-making. Between 1847 and 1869, her parents ran a coffee room and dining room at the Duke Street address, and later (1874-81) at 27 King Street, Portman Square.

In 1876 both girls were married, Lizzie to a William Kipps and Lucy to a pharmacist, Henry Peck. The Pecks' first home was 6 Derby Street, St Pancras, and there were two children of the marriage, which seems to have been a very happy one. Lucy's daughter, Ethel Frances Lucy (born August 1877), was the mother of my informant, and there was a son, Howard, born in 1882. No doubt her husband's knowledge assisted her in making her modelling materials, and also with some of her techniques. In 1893, with her children now aged 16 and 11, we find her setting up a prestigious shop at 131 Regent Street, and the "DOLLS' HOME," as it is proudly called, has a note to the effect that she has moved from Goodge Street. In the London Directory, she is listed at 5 Goodge Street with a Dolls' Warehouse from 1890 to 1892. The wax doll-makers Charles Edwards were at 16 Goodge Street, and so one wonders if there was some connection. Had Lucy worked or studied with them, perhaps?

The yearly premium for the Regent Street shop was £500, and the family lived over the shop. Photographs show just how fine a shop front Mrs Peck had, with broad windows on the corner of Heddon Street (still remaining) in a very fashionable quarter of London. One photograph (opposite) shows the "DOLLS' HOME" dressed in full regalia to celebrate Queen Victoria's Diamond Jubilee in 1897. One suspects that the celebrations must have been very good for trade in the famous toy shop with its patriotic bunting

Above Portrait of Mrs Lucy Peck. C.1895. (Mrs Norman-Smith)

and its fine displays of the Queen. One of Mrs Peck's specialities was portraits of the young Queen. These are sometimes wrongly dated and attributed. One of the most famous shows Victoria still quite a girl, in her nightgown with her long hair falling over her shoulders, when the news of her accession to the throne was brought to her in 1837. The doll echoes the famous picture by Mary Gow in the Royal Collection, Windsor. Unfortunately this doll, which originally belonged to Lucy Peck's daughter, was sold and has now been re-dressed in queenly regalia by a later hand.

The business in Regent Street lasted until the lease expired in 1908 and the last photograph shows the dismantled shop during its last sad days. It must have been a considerable wrench to Mrs Peck to leave. Writing a letter to a friend, she showed how much she had enjoyed her London site:

> Certainly you have more seclusion, magnificence and are altogether more flavoured [favoured?] with aristocracy if you take up your abode in Belgravia or its vicinity. But what is so delightful as a stroll down Regent St. on a sunny May morning? The throng, the shops, the broad, well-swept causeway – is there anything approaching to it for

Above The end of Mrs Peck's Dolls' Home in Regent Street, 1908. (Mrs Norman-Smith)

Right The Dolls' Home, Mrs Lucy Peck's shop at 131 Regent Street. (Mrs Norman-Smith)

an idler in all London? It is rather soon for the Park perhaps and, even if it were not, to your inveterate shop lounger Rotten Row is a comparatively dreary entertainment. But the Street – the noblest lounge in all the civilized world to which the grand Boulevard of Paris, or the Broad Way of New York are as nothing. There is always romance, a picture, a story or a jest to be found there. Much food for reflection to be got out of a walk up that regal promenade, take it when you will.

This extract is especially interesting, as it shows the sort of person Lucy Peck was and the type of society she enjoyed and moved in. Some of her wax dolls are beautifully dressed and perfectly represent late Victorian

fashions with wasp waist, flowing gown and delicate underclothes. Of course their feathered hats and pretty jewellery and little parasols are correct since they mirror the passing world outside their maker's shop.

The business was soon re-started further west at new quarters at 215 High Street, Kensington. An old account book from 1912 shows that Mrs Peck had lists of "Old Stock," presumably moved from the Regent Street shop. She sold a range of quite large toys there besides her own dolls, and the photographs show automata and doll prams, stuffed animals, dolls' houses and lanterns. In addition, she sold cards and pictures and quantities of Easter eggs. These were no doubt the bright chromolithographed cardboard type imported from Germany and made to hold a little gift, and were priced "card.eggs 2d. 3/6d, 4/9d (twopence, three shillings and sixpence, four shillings and ninepence)." From the many items one gains the feeling of a pretty shop crammed with small numbers of novelties as well as a few larger expensive toys and dolls. All sorts of stuffed animals were sold: a donkey and an elephant at six shillings and elevenpence, and parrots at three shillings and elevenpence. She seems to have done a steady trade in flags and of course various dolls. Her wax dolls were sold for one shilling and sixpence and model dolls for eight shillings and sixpence. Doll items included trousseau at four shillings and elevenpence, beads, workboxes, and heads and wigs at eight shillings and ninepence, plus dolls' furniture, baths, beds, clothes, hats, shoes and ear-rings. Some of these were no doubt hand-made, since she must have been an exquisite needlewoman and possibly also took on outside workers.

The collector's heart must miss a beat when we see that Mrs Peck was selling the Lehmann clockwork ostrich at one shilling and ninepence, named Jumeau dolls at sixteen shillings and elevenpence, and the newly introduced "flirting eye" or goo-goo doll at twelve shillings and sixpence.

There were a few boys' toys: a clockwork train set at seventeen shillings, wooden soldiers, a station at two shillings and sixpence and rails at one shilling.

Those prices of course meant something very different in 1912, when many folk took home no more than a £1 in wages each week and Mrs Peck herself seemed to make no more than £2 in an average week – not a very impressive profit given the amount sold each week.

By the outbreak of the First World War in 1914, Lucy Peck had moved again to 81 Wigmore Street, opening a "Dolls' Warehouse," and after the war she advertised a "Dolls' Hospital" at 306 Earls Court Road. Wax dolls had become unfashionable by then but a few were still being made, and early ones were in need of restoration. In 1916 her notebooks had carried details of "Shoulder heads without wigs" in three sizes – 1, 3 and 5 – at six shillings and ninepence, eight shillings and nine shillings and sevenpence, but these were probably replacement china heads. Heads and wigs and fair, blue eyes were available in sizes 9, 10 and 14 at fourteen shillings and tenpence, nineteen shillings and twopence and twenty-three shillings and sixpence. By 1922, Mrs Peck had retired from commerce, and for the last part of her life she lived first at Wimbledon and then at Kingston in south-west London, enjoying her hobby of clay modelling at Kingston Art School. At the end of her notebook, her husband Henry gently added: "All the foregoing was written by my dear wife Lucy Peck who died peacably on Monday October 20th. at 1 p.m. 1930."

It is especially interesting to find from an advertisement Mrs Peck designed that she also employed the services of another experienced wax doll-making family. From her description, it can have been none other than the Montanaris (see pages 83-95). Madame Augusta Montanari's son Richard Napoleon lived at 3 Rathbone Place, and since he seems to vanish from commercial records after 1886 he was probably working from his home premises and selling via the luxury toy shops in the West End. The advertisement specifically mentions the rag dolls for which Richard was famous and the 1851 Exhibition at which his parents won medals. It is interesting that Mrs Peck also mentions various sizes of golliwogg, as this kind of doll had become popular after the publication in 1895 of Florence Upton's book *The Dutch Dolls and Golliwogg*. A specimen is visible on the right of Mrs Peck's side window (see page 138).

Mrs Lucy Peck was in business at the end of the 19th century, when the popularity of wax dolls for play was beginning to fade and children wanted to own the more fashionable models made of bisque china. Mrs Peck herself stocked such dolls and examples from the Jumeau factory as well as her "old-fashioned" wax. But it does seem from the surviving models that she did an additional trade in model dolls, miniature mannequins that could be dressed in vogue or to represent an actual character.

One of the most intriguing of these miniature mannequins is shown on page 125, dressed to represent Evangeline, the heroine of a novel by the romantic novelist Elinor Glyn. In 1905, when she was 41 and already famous, Elinor Glyn published *The Vicissitudes of Evangeline* (published in the USA, perhaps wisely, under the title *Red Hair*). The novel reads quaintly in modern times and is a true 'period' piece of Edwardian *mores*. What is more interesting is that Evangeline is obviously a portrait of the author herself. The original edition of the book had a frontispiece showing

Right The beginning again at 215 Kensington High Street in 1911. (Mrs Norman-Smith)

Opposite This dressed wax doll by Lucy Peck represents Katherine Mary Noel-Hill on presentation at Court in 1902. She is known as "May." Her eyelashes are set in the upper lids, and hair is inserted in slits. Painted wax legs reach nearly to the thighs, and wax arms almost to the shoulders. There are grommets in the arms. This type of doll was sold for mannequin purposes. The doll is beautifully dressed by its owner. A Peck label reading "191 Regent Street" appears on the lower half of the body. (Mrs Graham Greene, Rotunda, Oxford)

a painted locket of Evangeline. This was rather an amateur effort done by May Dixon, the sister of Elinor Glyn's children's nurse "Dixie," and was copied from a little sketch Elinor herself made: a self-portrait with her head turned archly to one side, the flaming red hair draped with black chiffon and black ribbons and a flower at the corsage of the black gown. Elinor Glyn herself had red hair and green eyes, a milk white complexion and stately figure. In the novel Evangeline cries, "What a mercy black suits me!

My skin is ridiculously white – and I shall stick a bunch of violets in my frock." The doll costume bears this out and has in addition a splendid black straw hat with black feathers and trim of black sequins. Inside, the hat has a Paris label: "Louise Goure, 35 Rue Godot de Mauroy," near the Champs Elysées in the fashionable area of the city. It looks as if it was designed specifically for a doll and made exactly to size, perhaps to the order of Elinor Glyn who was often in Paris and did sketches of Parisian hats in her diaries. The one concession to fact is that the doll has blue eyes, whereas Evangeline says in the novel "My eyes are as green as pale emeralds…so you see I am branded as bad from the beginning." In simple fact, it was just not possible to acquire *green* doll's eyes. The beautiful long hair is human and is a startling red which looks as if it is fair hair dyed. It is plaited around the crown with a bun in the nape of the neck in the fashion Elinor herself affected.

Recipes from Lucy Peck's Notebooks:

To cast in Plaster of Paris
Use the finest and purest Plaster of Paris. When filling a mould learn to heat up the requisite quantity of cream quickly with care, to avoid making it too thick. In pouring this in use a good camel hair brush to prevent air bubbles: a mere surface of this thin cream is all that is required. While doing this have ready the thicker plaster of the consistency of light syrup and fill up the mould at once. In about *20 minutes* you can open the mould if your plaster is pure and has been properly mixed. If you do not put too much oil on the object to be moulded and have used your brush properly you will find clean sharp models.

Cream of tartar is used to retard setting of plaster.

Antique plaster casts can be restored by coating with a thin paste of starch; when partly dry, peel off.

[Note: Did Mrs Peck acquire some casts from earlier wax modellers?]

For hardening fibrous plaster, Litharge oil is composed of 1 lb. of litharge (oxide of lead) 1 lb Paraffin wax: ¾ of resin and 1 gallon linseed oil. Made in an iron pot over slow fire; the wax is melted in another pot and poured in. The litharge and resin are put in in a powdered state and constantly stirred.

As a substitute for Carton Pierre: 13 parts dissolved glue; 14 parts pulverised litharge; 8 parts white lead; 1 part plaster to 10 parts very fine sawdust.

Modelling Wax
Dissolve in pipkin (over slow fire) pure powdered beeswax; add 12th. part powdered resin; 10th of Venice Turpentine. Stir well. Don't let it boil. Add flake white until of desired consistency. Test plasticity by taking out a little and tell by working in hands.

Restoration and Modern Wax Doll-Making

Nineteenth-century dolls made either of poured wax or by wax over *papier-mâché* methods present the collector with problems of identification and conservation. None the less they are among the most interesting and desirable items, and often have a documented family history. On the other hand they are often anonymous – that is, they are not actually marked with the marker's signature or the stamp of the shop where they were sold. Frequently they have often deteriorated from their original very pretty condition, so much in many cases that their costumes are more interesting than the doll itself, which may have become painfully hideous!

What should one do? Most old dolls will benefit from a careful spring-clean. But take care not to touch the actual fabric of the wax. Beyond that, it is always more desirable to call in the help of a professional wax doll-restorer. A few modern makers both in Britain and the USA have resurrected the art of wax-modelling. Employing the original techniques and materials used by Victorian makers like those artists with their "Dolls' Hospitals," they are the ones best qualified to carry out careful repairs and replacements.

Modern artists in wax do not aim to make reproduction dolls imitating the Victorian models of Montanari or Pierotti. They study early methods and use their own casts and moulds to produce original wax dolls for collectors. Mrs Margaret Glover of Isleworth in west London, for instance, has made various very beautiful replicas of such famous characters as "Bubbles" – the little boy blowing soap bubbles long used to advertise Pear's Soap. (The original painting was by Millais of the little son of Augustus John.) Mrs Glover uses wax heads and limbs on a fabric body and then dresses the models herself. She has also produced Renoir's little girl with a hoop and his little girl with a watering can and recently the famous *Puss in Boots* picture, also by Millais, of a child playing with a kitten wearing her doll's bootees. Such work will certainly find its place among the antiques of the future.

Margaret Glover undertakes much restoration and repair of fine old wax dolls, and stresses how important it is for an owner to retain the broken pieces and original fabric and costume of an early doll to serve as guidelines for replacement. Many of her worst repair jobs are those in which an amateur has already attempted the work with inadequate tools and materials. It is very important to match the texture and colour of wax, and it is no simple matter to simulate work done perhaps a hundred years ago. The model shown on page 128 by Mrs Glover is of A.A. Milne's Christopher Robin – *not* of course, one should insist, the Christopher Robin of Walt Disney! – in his original smock clothing and with his beloved friends Pooh and Piglet.

Detail of a Princess Louise model doll shown at the London Exhibition in
1853. 14½ inches. (Bethnal Green Museum of Childhood)

Chronological Directory of Wax Doll-Makers

At the beginning of the 19th century, a wide area of London to the east of the centre (Shoreditch, Hoxton, Clerkenwell) was devoted to small trades that supplied the luxury shops being set up in the West End. There were watch-makers, craftsmen in jewellery and trinkets, and there, too, were the doll-makers. By the middle of the century, shops and makers were closer in to the centre of London at Holborn and Soho. By mid-century, there were also doll-making workshops south of the river Thames (see the map on the endpapers for more detailed information).

1818	John Stubbs, 25 Brownlow Street, Holborn. Wax and "wachee" (wax over) dolls.
1820	Mary Stubbs (John Stubbs' widow?), 19 Kingsgate Street, Holborn.
1823/24	Anthony Bazzoni, 17 Kingsgate Street, Holborn. Became famous as the maker of the "speaking doll."
1826	Charles Butler, 18 Aylesbury, Clerkenwell and Exmouth Market. (Address in 1844, 6 St John's Square, Clerkenwell.)
1826	Mrs Ann Santy, 131 Fleet Street, and Soho Bazaar. Milliner.
1826	Benjamin Gay, Goswell Street, E.C.
1826	John Naylor, Hoxton Market.
1827	Joseph Evans (warehouse) 5 Newgate Street, London. E.C. Evans & Sons (shop), 1868-81, 114/116 Newgate Street, London E.C.
1834	John Dominic Pierotti, 21 Gower Place, Bedford Square.
1835	Anthony Bazzoni, 128 High Holborn. Wholesale Doll and Toyman.
1843	Robert Ogilwy, 54 Tabernacle Walk, E. (From 1852 to 1856 worked with George Teather in composition and waxed composition dolls.)
1843	James Brogden, 5 Cross Street, Hatton Garden.
1843	Douglas & Hamer, 56 Shoe Lane, E.C. Succeeded by William Hamer, 1848.
1844	William Wheelhouse, 1 Sandy's Brow, Bishopsgate. Wax dolls.
1845	Mary Ann Pierotti, Milliner, 7 Judd Street, Brunswick Square. Then 92 Charlotte Street, Fitzroy Square, until 1852.
1847	John Barton, 2 Constitution Road, Gray's Inn Road. Wax dolls.
1848	Richard Montanari, Modeller, 52 Frith Street, Soho.
1849	Appears as Napoleon Montanari, Waxworks, Regent Street.
1852-54	Appears as Napoleon Montanari, 29 Upper Charlotte Street.
1855-62	Appears as Napoleon Montanari, 13 Charles Street, Soho.
1853	Charles Edwards, 16 Goode Street, Tottenham Court Road, W.

John and Mrs Shields, 11 Mount Street, Lambeth.

Henry Pierotti, 32 Great Ormond Street, Queen Square.

J.D. Pierotti, 8 Argyle Street, Kings Cross, Doll-maker.

1853-81	William Rich, 14 Great Russell Street. Wax dolls and models.
1855	Mme Augusta Montanari, 13 Charles Street, Soho. Model wax dolls.
1855	Herbert John Meech, 16 York Place, Westwood Road. Wax figure-maker.
1855	Mrs Snowball.
1855	Joseph Thorpe. Wax doll-maker.
1855	Thomas Bluett, 1 Nelson Square, Blackfriar's Road. Wax and composition dolls.
1855-65	John Hobbins, 47 Market Street, Borough Road. Wax dolls.
1857-65	William and Charles Wheelhouse, 31 Waterloo Road, S.E. Wax and wax-over dolls.
1862	W.H. Cremer, German Toy Warehouse, Bond Street. Then W.H. Cremer and Son, toy shop, 210 Regent Street until 1873. English and imported wax dolls, doll-maker.
1862	William Peacock and Sons, "The Beaming Nurse" toyshop, 525 New Oxford Street (corner of Bloomsbury Street), until 1911.
1862	Henry Pierotti, 13 Mortimer Street.
1864	William Marsh, 28 Union Street, Middlesex Hospital. Wax dolls.
1864	Charles Marsh, 102 Bolsover Street, Fitzroy Square. (Sold dolls at Soho Bazaar with C. Gooch and E. Moody.)
1864	William Wheelhouse, 63 Sun Street, Bishopsgate Street.
1865	James Wheelhouse, 31 Waterloo Road, London S.E.
1866	Napoleon Montanari, 198 Oxford Street.
1868	Charles and Henrietta Edwards, 40 Goodge Street.
1868	John Edwards, 41/43 Waterloo Road.
1868	Herbert John Meech, 50/52 Kennington Road.

Joseph Evans, 114/116 Newgate Street, London, E.C. Dealer in dolls until 1881.

1868-94	William Pitfield, 17 de Beauvoir Crescent, N. Wax dolls.
1870-90	Silber and Fleming, 57 Wood Street, London. Large-scale wholesalers stocking wax dolls made in Britain and Europe.
1870	Horace W. Morrell, 50 Burlington Arcade (a toy shop since about 1820).

Like Cremer's, Morrell's famous toy shop stamped its own name on the fabric body of wax dolls bought from makers such as Pierotti and Marsh. The shop started at 50 Burlington Arcade in about 1870 by Horace W. Morrell was continued there by his wife Jane Arundel and his son Charles on his death. They had started in business in 1880 at 164 Oxford Street, and moved in 1894 to 368 Oxford Street. By 1922 the shop in Burlington Arcade was run by his grandsons Frank and Richard.

1865	Charles Marsh, 102 Bulsover Street, Fitzroy Square, and also at the Corinthian Bazaar. Sold dolls at the Soho Bazaar through C. Gooch and E. Moody.
1876-83	Jane and Celia Pierotti, Baker Street Bazaar (Portman Rooms).

1876-1900	Edward Smith, "The City Toyshop," 8 Cheapside. Wax dolls, etc.
1876-1900	Frederick Aldis, 61, 63 and 65 Buckingham Palace Road and 10-13 Belgrave Mansions. Doll-maker and -importer.
1878	Henrietta Edwards, 35 Goodge Street.
1879-1912	Thomas Betts and Marion Betts, 150 St John's Road, Hoxton; 12 de Beauvoir Road, N. Wax and composition dolls.
1880	Charles Morrell and Mrs Jane Arundel Morrell, Doll Warehouse, 164 Oxford Street, and then 50 Burlington Arcade.
1880-1903	Thomas Aldred. Doll-maker and -importer.
1881	Walter Stiff, 181 Goswell Road. Made and exported wax dolls.
1887	Thomas Betts, 12 de Beauvoir Road, N.
1887	Charles and Mary Ann Marsh, 114 Fulham Road, S.W.
1887	Julius Ephraimson, 35 Jewin Crescent, E. Manufacturer of doll hair and wigs.
1890	Mrs Lucy Peck, 5 Goodge Street. Wax dolls and models.
1893	Mrs Lucy Peck, "The Dolls' Home", 131 Regent Street. Hamley Brothers, Toy Warehouse, Regent Street. Richard Montanari, 3, Rathbone Place. Maker of wax dolls and London rag babies.
1894	Mary Ann Marsh (presumed widow), 114 Fulham Road, S.W.
1911	Miss Jessica Marsh, Dolls' Hospital, 114 Fulham Road.
1911	Mrs Lucy Peck, 215 Kensington High Street.
1911-20	James and William Wheelhouse.
1925	Miss M. Wheelhouse.

In 1876, George Bartley (see page 133) reported that about 16 wax doll-makers were working in London. Nothing is known about some of the makers in the list above, which has been compiled from directories, other than their name and address. But it is always possible that a marked example may turn up to fill in our knowledge about the type of work they did.

Identification Tables

Most makers of poured wax dolls worked over a long period with various members of their family, using employees for the less skilled areas of their work. It is impossible to generalize about the work they produced, since they changed the moulds and materials through the years and also turned out a variety of quality, size and value of doll model. In the chart that follows, I have listed a few characteristics that may help to identify wax and wax-over dolls. The collector's best guide always is to view actual examples in museums or auction sales, since no description quite conveys a doll's personality.

MAKER (OR TYPE)

Religious dolls
Small wax character dolls for dolls houses

SIZE AND COLOUR	CONSTRUCTION DETAILS	TRADE MARK OR SIGNATURE
Made in all sizes very small to very large. Early, pure beeswax dolls, often very browned.	Distinguished by "spiritual" appearance. Often encased, decked with flowers or presented in ornamental cradle. Wax figures were made in all Roman Catholic countries and widely used for *crèche* scenes.	Various European makers, usually unidentified: French or German.

MAKER (OR TYPE)

Early French fashion 18th century and earlier.

SIZE AND COLOUR	CONSTRUCTION DETAILS	TRADE MARK OR SIGNATURE
Usually small size for transport but history records full-size "Pandoras." Prettily tinted wax, glass eyes, shaped bust.	Fine-quality wax used for head/bust and arms of poured wax. Often over a framework of wood or bound wire to support elaborate costume. Painted features, hair wig.	PARIS. Various.

	MAKER (OR TYPE)	
	18th/19th-century wax "split-head" German peg-wooden.	

SIZE AND COLOUR	CONSTRUCTION DETAILS	TRADE MARK OR SIGNATURE
Usually 10–12 inches. Possibly made in smaller and larger sizes.	Pretty features, glass eyes worked by wire. Real hair inserted in central slit of parting. Skilful jointed wooden construction.	Probably Sonneberg.

	MAKER (OR TYPE)	
	"Bazaar" dolls, "Bagman's Baby" (small cheap dolls sold by pedlars and hawkers).	

SIZE AND COLOUR	CONSTRUCTION DETAILS	TRADE MARK OR SIGNATURE
Small, cheap dolls either of one-mould wax or wax-over *papier-mâché* head on crude stitched body.	Often of "cottage industry" construction or back-room London industry. Also little mechanical novelties.	Various. Hawkers' wares.

Santy. Inventor
340 Long Room
Soho. Bazaar
London

	MAKER (OR TYPE)	
	Cheap London wax-over *papier-mâché* or carton (laminate), first half of 19th century.	

SIZE AND COLOUR	CONSTRUCTION DETAILS	TRADE MARK OR SIGNATURE
Large size, usually 24–36 inches. Colourful features painted beneath wax coating. Pleasant expression. Blue, brown or grey glass eyes.	Fabric body, hair wig pinned to round hollow crown. Usually wire-eyed sleeping movement, with wire emerging at crutch or side. Sawdust filled. Arms and legs wax-over or stitched kid arms and "pigeon-toed" fabric legs.	Clerkenwell makers such as Butler; Butler signature. Signature of Santy, doll-maker, Soho Bazaar. 1860.

	MAKER (OR TYPE)	
	BAZZONI	

SIZE AND COLOUR	CONSTRUCTION DETAILS	TRADE MARK OR SIGNATURE
Little known, but he made large, expensive dolls.	Famous for doll with "speaking" apparatus. No example known. Single known example of marked Bazzoni doll (see page 71).	Stamp.

German wax-over from Sonneberg. Sometimes called "squash-head" or "pumpkin-head" from yellow moulded hair type. Also "bonnet-head."

SIZE AND COLOUR	CONSTRUCTION DETAILS	TRADE MARK OR SIGNATURE
Small, 9 inches to large, 30 inches. Dark pupil-less eyes. 	Various patterns often with details of hair, ornaments, ribbons, bonnets, hats moulded in *papier-mâché* beneath wax complete with colour and features. Wooden arms and legs or composition arms and legs decorated with sock and shoe. Stuffed with moss, hay or sawdust.	A vast industry producing often unmarked dolls. Trademark of Cremer shop, 1870. Very many makers in Sonneberg. Type of painted, carved wooden foot (Sonneberg dolls). Type of painted, decorated composition foot (German). *Holzmasse* mark. Dressel. *Holzmasse* mark of famous firm of C. & O. Dressel, Sonneberg (see page 108).

"Mottschmann" type.

SIZE AND COLOUR	CONSTRUCTION DETAILS	TRADE MARK OR SIGNATURE
Small, 8 inches, to large, 30 inches.	Baby doll or *Taufling* (see page 126) made after style of Japanese dolls with "floating" limbs. Cylinder leg and arm wooden pieces. "Ski" foot. Voice squeaker, either concertina or press type. 	Sonneberg, 1850 period Mottschmann 1857 (patent). The "Mottschmann" type leg of *Taufling* dolls with "ski-pant" cylinder.

PIEROTTI family

SIZE AND COLOUR	CONSTRUCTION DETAILS	TRADE MARK OR SIGNATURE
Small to large and also figurines and life-size models, busts etc. Realistic colouring but some later dolls made by this family have a characteristic "shrimp" pink. *Pierotti*	Invented royal model baby – not the prettiest but indisputably royal with pale blue eyes, sparse, fair hair, high forehead. Head often slightly gazing to side, plump neck and groove indicated between shoulder blades. Finger nails and toe nails engraved. The fabric body waisted and not babyish and the legs moulded straight and shapely. Later baby model with pretty "Pierotti" features, Titian hair and curved limbs. Charles Ernest, a clever sculptor, made models of King Edward VII and his generals, beautifully costumed.	Occasionally scratched PIEROTTI at hair line, back of neck. Also various shop names stamped on dolls – Peacock, Aldis, Cremer, Hamley, Morrell. Pierotti mark rarely scratched in wax. Usually unsigned but clearly Pierotti work.

MONTANARI family

SIZE AND COLOUR	CONSTRUCTION DETAILS	TRADE MARK OR SIGNATURE
Large dolls in poured wax and also exhibition figurines. Napoleon was originally a wax-figure maker. *Montanari*	Early dolls have inserted hair (usually in slit insert), but single needle used for special work. (The "eye" of the needle was broken off and that end used to pierce hair in to wax.) Wax modelling probably done by Napoleon, but Augusta was a genius with millinery. She used expensive material, ribbons, lace, fringe, seed pearls, ornaments. Doll dress she favoured was 1850s style V-shaped yoke. Dolls had rather heavy features, dark hair, even teeth. Plump limbs with crease at wrist and elbow.	Some early dolls have Montanari ink signature on fabric base of torso. Later "rag" dolls often have 1851 Great Exhibition gold medal seal. Soho Bazaar Dolls often sold in strong wooden box. Montanari, ink signature on fabric of dolls.

	MAKER (OR TYPE)	
	Montanari, Richard Napoleon	
SIZE AND COLOUR	CONSTRUCTION DETAILS	TRADE MARK OR SIGNATURE
London rag doll about 12 to 14 inches	Specialized in baby doll made with wax or muslin mask framed by lacy bonnet.	Possibly also modelled for Mrs Lucy Peck (later period).

	MAKER (OR TYPE)	
	MEECH family	
SIZE AND COLOUR	CONSTRUCTION DETAILS	TRADE MARK OR SIGNATURE
Medium-sized poured wax dolls. Also busts for hair-dressers etc. Wax rather pale but fine quality and modelling. 13, 21 and 24 inches.	Meech dolls seem to bear a family likeness: strong rather sulky features; fine eyes and tooled lids. Inserted eye lashes and thick eyebrows. Luxurious human hair. Tinted sculpted lips. Hands have closed fingers, dimpled knuckles, marked "life-line" one palm. Millinery of original clothes very special. One detail is little shoulder bows. (Many dolls survive re-dressed and repaired.)	Meech dolls usually marked with rubber stamp. Claimed as doll-maker to the royal family, probably King Edward VII. Trademark of H J Meech.

H·J·MEECH
DOLLS CLEANED & REPAIRED
50 KENNINGTON ROAD.
LONDON. S·E·1·

	MAKER (OR TYPE)	
	MARSH family	
SIZE AND COLOUR	CONSTRUCTION DETAILS	TRADE MARK OR SIGNATURE
Wax tinted, pretty pink. Of all the makers produced a "dolly" effect to his models with wide eyes, a straight look and strong construction. Recorded as selling dolls to the USA.	Marsh dolls seem to have a definite neck and head held rather erect. Hair often mohair inserted in tufts and centre-marked parting and Alice ribbon. The hands frequently have divided fingers and special attention was paid to the moulding of ears. Marsh seems to have produced "little girl" models, not babies.	Pronounced himself sole manufacturer. Most dolls have name stamp and in addition sometimes name of distributor. Dolls' hospital run for repairs. Trademark of Chas. Marsh.

CHAS MARSH
SOLE MANUFACTURER
LONDON · W.
DOLLS &c REPAIRED

MAKER (OR TYPE)

EDWARDS family

SIZE AND COLOUR	CONSTRUCTION DETAILS	TRADE MARK OR SIGNATURE
Known dolls rather pale in colour but well modelled. Edwards advertised that he made dolls copied from well-known paintings and also mechanical dolls. A lot remains to be discovered about this maker.	Edwards dolls are largely unidentified, since he did not add a name mark. But one should look carefully among the unmarked dolls since his output was very large. Also used weighted eyes in some models.	Models known by Exhibition entry. Cipher used on doll shoe for Edwards. Advertised that he made wax and wax-over composition. Inventor of the exhibition wax model. Edwards cipher E stamped on bottom of doll shoe.

FROM
MRS. PECK
THE DOLL'S HOME
131 REGENT STREET
— W —

MAKER (OR TYPE)

Mrs Lucy Peck

SIZE AND COLOUR	CONSTRUCTION DETAILS	TRADE MARK OR SIGNATURE
Advertised that she used services of a famous wax modeller from the 1851 Exhibition – perhaps Richard Napoleon Montanari? Her range of dolls varies so much that she herself perhaps made play dolls and employed Pierotti and Montanari for some of her fashion figures.	Large handsome play dolls in poured wax with glass eyes. Some had old-style wire opening eye apparatus. Beautiful elegant dolls for fashionable figure representation. Very fine costume and coiffure.	Used name stamp at her Regents Street address and also at Kensington. Trade mark of Mrs Lucy Peck "Dolls' Home."

Bibliography

Books

Altick, Richard, *Shows of London* (1978, Bellsnap Press, Harvard)

Boehn, Max von, *Dolls and Puppets* (1932, London; translation)

Cadbury, Betty, *Playthings Past* (1976, David and Charles, Newton Abbott)

Coleman, Dorothy S., Elizabeth A., and Evelyn J., *Collector's Book of Doll Clothes* (1975, Crown Publishing, New York)

Coleman, Dorothy S., Elizabeth A., and Evelyn J., *Collector's Encyclopedia of Dolls* (1968, Crown Publishing, New York)

Crane, Eva, *A Book of Honey* (1980, Oxford University Press, Oxford)

Dolls Collectors' Manual (1967, Doll Collectors of America, Inc.)

Early, Alice K., *English Dolls, Effigies and Puppets* (1955, B. T. Batsford, London)

Fraser, H. Malcolm, *Beekeeping in Antiquity* (1931, University of London Press, London)

Gerken, Jo E. Clay, *Wonderful Dolls of Papier Mâché* (1970, Doll Research Associates, Lincoln, Nebraska)

Gerken, Jo E. Clay, *Wonderful Dolls of Wax* (1964, Calico Print Shop, Wichita, Kansas)

Handmaid of the Arts (1796, London; 2 parts)

Hillier, Mary, *Dolls and Dollmakers* (1968, Weidenfeld & Nicolson, London)

Hillier, Mary (ed.), *Pollock's Dictionary of English Dolls* (1982, Robert Hale, London)

Jackson, F. N., *Toys of Other Days* (1908, London)

Jacobs, Flora Gill, *A History of Dolls' Houses* (1965, Charles Scribner's Sons, New York)

King, Constance Eileen, *The Collector's History of Dolls* (1977, Robert Hale, London)

Leslie, Anita and Chapman, Pauline, *Madame Tussaud* (1978, Hutchinson, London)

Longford, Elizabeth, *Victoria, R. I.* (1964, Weidenfeld & Nicolson, London)

Matéaux, C. L. *Wonderland of Work* (1883, Cassell, London)

Peter Parley's Annual (1867, London)

Pyke, E. J., *A Biographical Dictionary of Wax Modellers* and supplements (1973, Oxford University Press, Oxford)

Timbs, J., *Curiosities of London* (1868, London)

White, Gwen, *European and American Dolls* (1966, B. T. Batsford, London)

Periodicals

Doll Reader, Illustrated London News, Little Folks, The Morning Chronicle, Queen, Strand Magazine

Index